BROOKE COUGHLIN

SHE CLOSES DEALS

Become a *million-dollar real estate agent*
& build your ***dream life***

The information contained in this book is for general informational purposes only and should not be construed as financial or legal advice. The author and publisher make no guarantees regarding the accuracy, completeness, or timeliness of the information presented. It is highly recommended that you consult with a qualified financial advisor and/or attorney for specific guidance and advice relevant to your individual circumstances. You are solely responsible for your investment and business decisions based on your situation and risk tolerance.

First paperback edition 2024
Interior Formatting by 100Covers.
ISBN 9798328117180 (paperback)

Table of Contents

Dedication

I am honored, proud, and humbled to release this book to the world. It wouldn't be possible without the support of many incredible people. This book is dedicated to those who have helped me thrive.

My deepest gratitude goes to the Byrnes Real Estate Group for allowing me to be part of their thriving brokerage and fostering my professional growth. Mike Byrnes, your mentorship has taken me to a level I couldn't have imagined even a few years ago. Lisa, your knowledge and guidance have been invaluable—you seem to have the answer to every question I throw your way. And Emily, thank you for keeping me organized and on top of things.

A big shout-out to my friends at Flynn Law and my trusted lenders, Katya Magee and Joey Padilla. I also want to thank Cody Berman, Julie Berninger, and Taylor Smith from the incredible team at Auros Agency for helping me write this book. Your support has been instrumental in taking my business to the next level.

To all of my amazing clients who have also become friends, thank you for your trust and continued support. I hope I'll always be the one you call for your real estate needs.

Finally, to my incredible husband, thank you for your unwavering support and for taking on the cooking duties at home! And to my family who always believes in me tenfold, your encouragement has been invaluable.

Success is truly about the team around you, and I am deeply grateful for each and every one of you. Teamwork truly does make the dream work!

I am living my absolute dream in this industry!

Introduction

Not too long ago, I was a teacher making $50,000 and stuck in a classroom every day. Now, I've sold over $100,000,000 worth of real estate. It doesn't happen overnight, but if you don't start, it doesn't happen at all.

I am so happy you're here, and that you're holding this book. This is your first step into living a life of financial freedom, having a flexible schedule, and becoming a successful real estate agent who closes millions in deals every year.

If you pulled up my instagram (@brookeecoughlin) right now, you'd see that I am a top realtor in Massachusetts, Connecticut, and Rhode Island, a multi-million dollar real estate investor, owner of a thriving cleaning company and co-owner of an Airbnb business. But before I embarked on this exciting journey, I was a dedicated seventh-grade teacher who loved her students but was looking for a way out and a way to build a better life on my own terms.

The truth is, my foray into real estate wasn't exactly planned. It began with a chance encounter during a cleaning job. I was giving a quote to the homeowners, and showing them what my cleaning company does and how much it would cost, and the homeowners abruptly interrupted me and asked, "Do you have any interest in real estate?"

Surprised by the question, but also curious, I said that I enjoyed looking at houses and browsing on Realtor.com and Zillow but that was about it. The homeowner said, "You would be amazing at real estate." Little did I know, this client was in the real estate industry. It was this one encounter that would change my life and open up an entire world of opportunities.

Intrigued, I decided to get my license and the agents I met that first day helped walk me through it. While initially hesitant about making it my full-time gig, my brain was also working overtime thinking about how amazing it would be to not have to work my rigid teaching schedule, how I could build my own brand, vacation whenever I wanted, and make a lot more money than my teaching salary.

My journey to becoming a real estate agent, however, was anything but smooth. I am possibly the worst test-taker in the history of test-taking. When it came to passing my teacher's exam, it took me five attempts, and that was just the beginning. I failed my real estate licensing exam so many times I actually stopped counting after a while.

I would walk into the real estate exam testing center and the woman at the front desk knew me by name. Each visit was a painful reminder of my previous failures. I felt compelled to announce to her, "Hi, it's Brooke, I'm back again!" smiling so she hopefully couldn't see how embarrassed I was.

There are two parts to the real estate licensing exam in Massachusetts, and you have to pass both within a certain time frame or you have to start all over again. I would pass the first one but fail the second. It was a grueling process, taking me between eight to ten attempts to pass both sections of the exam.

But looking back, I realize that the test itself wasn't the most important part. Most of the real estate exam content does not directly correlate with being a successful real estate agent. What mattered was the persistence and resilience I developed through the process.

When I finally passed, I remember telling the woman at the test center, "I hope I never see you again." Of course, I ended up returning to the same testing center for my broker's exam, but by then, she was no longer there.

This journey taught me a valuable lesson: persistence is key. It's not about how many times you fall, but how many times you get back up. My path to becoming a real estate agent was full of setbacks, but I'm not one to give up. My determination led me to a career filled with challenges, rewards, and the chance to build something truly special.

This book is an extension of that journey. Here, I'll share my experiences, insights, and the knowledge I've gained to help you navigate your own path in the exciting world of real estate. If you are a newly licensed agent, an agent looking to take your game to the next level, or someone looking to make a pivot into a career with more flexibility and income potential, I'm here to help lead the way.

The Five Lessons I've Learned

I've learned a lot since I started my real estate journey. These five lessons have stuck with me and can help to set expectations and decide if this is the path for you.

1. It's not entirely glamorous.

Let's be honest, the world of real estate can seem very glamorous from the outside. Think sleek suits, million-dollar listings, and the thrill of the close. But before you get swept away by the *Selling Sunset* portrayal, let's get real. While the potential for success and financial freedom is undeniably real, it's not all smooth sailing.

One of the things I wish I'd known when I started was that it takes time to become successful. You're going to spend a lot of time and money before you make money. Most people give up way too soon, because they want to make a quick dollar. I never approached real estate trying to get paid fast.

I wanted to make a lot of money over the course of my career, so I was willing to invest the time and energy. I have a feeling you also want to build a legacy of time and financial freedom for yourself (and maybe your family), which is why you're reading this book.

So, you might be wondering, why now is an opportune moment to embark on a career in real estate? Well, it all boils down to opportunity, flexibility, and the chance to make a real difference. Whether you enter the real estate industry when it's a buyer's market or a seller's market really doesn't matter. Real estate is full of opportunities, no matter the market. And the people who don't quit? The ones who keep going for as long as it takes? *They can make hundreds of thousands to millions of dollars each year.*

2. Real estate is for you if you genuinely care about helping people.

Imagine the satisfaction of helping a young couple buy their first home, or the excitement of helping a family find the perfect investment property, or the privilege of assisting retirees in downsizing and embarking on their next chapter. As a real estate agent, you're not just facilitating transactions; you're playing a pivotal role in people's lives, leaving a lasting impact on their journeys. The real estate business is a people business.

3. There are no limits on how much money you can make.

The potential for earning in real estate is *uncapped*. This was one reason I went all in on real estate and ultimately left my teaching career. I will never be capped by an employer's salary again. Your income is directly tied to your effort and expertise, allowing you to build a career that reflects your dedication and hard work.

4. You can create your dream schedule.

As a real estate agent, you can create a daily schedule that complements your lifestyle, manage your workload with autonomy, and achieve a work-life balance that suits your needs. Whether you're a morning person or a night owl, a social butterfly or a self-starter, real estate allows you to design a work environment that empowers you to perform at your best.

5. You can specialize and you have endless opportunities.

The real estate industry is a vast and dynamic landscape. You have so many options. You can dive into residential real estate, commercial properties, vacation rentals, investment properties, property management, flipping houses, foreclosures, wholesaling, or a mix of these. There are always new opportunities waiting to be explored, which makes for an exciting career.

When I talk to other women about real estate, I am often asked these three questions. So I want to cover them in case you have doubts about whether or not this career makes sense for you.

Is Real Estate Right for You?

Despite what you see on TV, you don't need to look or act like the cast of Selling Sunset in order to become a successful real estate agent. This job welcomes individuals from all walks of life and career stages. Whether you're a recent graduate or someone looking to make a career change, real estate is available to you.

As someone who receives questions from aspiring agents on the daily, here are the two most common questions I receive, and my honest answers.

"What skills do I need to be successful?"

Communication, negotiation, problem-solving, and adaptability are key. One thing I wish I had known as a brand new agent is that everything in real estate is negotiable—from working with a brokerage to working with clients to working with other agents. We'll dive into more of these types of negotiations throughout the book!

Real estate also requires you to be able to talk to everyone and anyone. You'll learn how to walk into a room and talk to people you've never met and walk out with connections and potential clients.

You also need to be able to sell anything. Selling is difficult for most people, but with practice, anyone can do it. All of these skills can be honed and developed through training, experience, and a commitment to continuous learning.

"Can I balance work and life as a real estate agent?"

One of the beautiful things about real estate is that you can create a work-life balance that aligns with your needs. You can work part time or full time, take personal time off, work from home, or structure your work schedule however you need to. You need effective time management, organization, and the support of a strong network, but you *can* make this happen.

Whether you're a woman in your early 20s, a single mom, a working parent, someone who's never owned a home, or considering a career change—you can succeed. The same goes for those starting over, coming from a non real estate background, or facing any situation that might make you hesitate. There are thousands of successful women in real estate who prove it's possible.

There are always ways to make real estate work for you. You'll set your own schedule, fill your knowledge gaps, and find a support system to help you. It will be a little messy, and you will make mistakes, but as long as you are committed, you can become a successful agent.

Change = Opportunity

Real estate is a field that never sleeps. The industry is always changing and presenting new opportunities. As agents, we are always "on." With ever-evolving market trends, emerging technologies, and shifting regulations, you'll constantly be challenged to learn and adapt. If you are someone who likes doing and learning new things, you'll find yourself constantly growing both personally and professionally.

At the time of writing this book, the real estate industry is going through massive changes with real estate commissions. And where there is change, there is opportunity.

Changes in Commissions

Commissions are the percentage of the final sale price of a property that agents are paid in exchange for their services in the real estate transaction. In other words, the commission is how much you receive as a payment when you close a deal. The exact percentage is negotiable and can vary depending on the market and the terms of your agreement.

Agent commissions have been somewhat controversial for decades. The National Association of Realtors (NAR) recently settled a lawsuit that is changing the way that commissions are paid out to agents.[1] Up to this point, both the buyer's and seller's agents' commissions have generally been paid by the sellers. While buyer's agents' commissions were technically "negotiable" by law, in practice, they were generally presented to buyers and their agents as "set" by sellers. Now, sellers can no longer include the buyer's agent commission they are willing to pay in the MLS listing details.

Under the new rules, everything is up for negotiation in a way that is more transparent for buyers. Buyers can ask for sellers to pay for their agent's commission (note: sellers are not required to pay), they can split the commission with sellers, or they will be responsible for paying their own agents at closing. At the time of writing this book, financing a realtor's commission directly into a mortgage isn't typically allowed.[2] There may be some lenders who allow buyers to finance agent commissions, but it's not a widely accepted practice. However, it is possible lending rules will shift in the near future as a result of the NAR settlement.

Buyer's Agent Opportunities

Previously, agents were marketed to buyers as "free" (not out-of-pocket costs) before the NAR settlement. Since clients are now paying for the agent's services, it is now more important than ever for buyers to work with a top agent. Clients will want to get the most out of their investment. Buyer's agents, you are now your client's most valuable asset in the deal!

Any time you are representing a buyer, you will be impacted by the new rule change. It is an opportunity to potentially earn even more as the buyer's agent. If you have good negotiating skills, this change will allow you as the buyer's agent to potentially earn more than you would if the commission was set by the seller's agent on the MLS. For example, if the conventional buyer's agent commission set on the MLS was 2 percent, buyer's agents can now charge 2.5–3 percent for their top-tier services.

While you can now potentially earn more through skilled negotiation, your true focus should always be on maximizing value for your client. Your expertise in navigating the market, identifying undervalued properties, and negotiating the best possible terms can save your buyer tens of thousands of dollars on the purchase price. Think of it this way: a higher commission for you translates to a significantly lower overall cost for your client, making your service an exceptional investment.

Educating Clients

We will now have to educate our clients about these changes. It will be important to have honest, upfront conversations with buyers and let them know that sellers are not obligated to pay buyer's agent fees. NAR agents are now also required to have written agreements with buyers in order to use the MLS system.[1]

As a buyer's agent, I will advise my clients that when we put in offers, we will first ask sellers to pay the buyer's agent commission, but the sellers can decline to do so. I also have room to negotiate this in the deal. For example, I can propose that the sellers pay 1percent of my commission and my buyers pay the remaining 1 percent commission.

Since sellers will likely no longer have to agree to pay the full commission, I explain to my buyers that they will need to pay for my services in the event that the sellers do not agree to pay my commission, and I set a minimum 2 percent commission as a buyer's agent.

Flexibility is Key

Ultimately, we don't know how much the new rules from the NAR settlement will shift or change the real estate industry.

Home buyers may start looking for alternative options to commissions. Some buyers may be interested in flat-fee agreements, where you set a fixed upfront fee for your services regardless of the final sale price. This can be attractive to buyers targeting a specific price range. There's also the possibility of performance-based compensation, where your fee is partially tied to the savings you achieve for the buyer on the purchase price. The type of clients you primarily work with (for example: First-time homebuyers vs. investors) may ultimately define your future commission structure, but we'll talk more about working with different clients throughout this book.

Changes in the industry are inevitable. And if changes are inevitable, the best way to approach them is to be flexible and see every change as an opportunity. By honing your negotiation skills and becoming an indispensable advocate for your clients, you can not only thrive in this new environment but also stand out as a trusted advisor, ensuring your success and empowering your clients to achieve their homeownership dreams.

Chapter 1
In Your Real Estate Era

"Finding opportunity is a matter of believing it's there." - Barbara Corcoran[1]

Imagine living a life where every morning you wake up filled with excitement, knowing that the day ahead is aligned with your passions and goals. You quickly check your phone for beautiful new homes on the market and send them over to your top buyers before making a smoothie for breakfast and going for a long walk with your dog.

You take your time getting ready, doing your luxurious skin-care routine, and then head to your office, respond to clients' questions, and send over your questionnaire to new leads that have come in overnight. You hop in your Range Rover, hit the road for showings, an open house, and then dinner with your partner at a nice restaurant.

You're celebrating that you closed over $1 million in deals this month already, and over a shared slice of cheesecake and a glass of rosé, you plan out your next vacay together. That night, curled up in bed, you book your flights and luxury resort, and you're not worried about the cost.

When I was a teacher, this is what I pictured my dream day would look like as a real estate agent. This wasn't just a dream; I knew it was a real possibility.

Once I started diving into real estate, I just started getting more and more excited. I was obsessed. I couldn't stop thinking about it. I was visualizing owning multiple properties, going on vacations, selling millions of dollars worth of deals, and leaving my job as a teacher for good.

Your dream life doesn't have to look like mine or anyone else's. Maybe it's having the flexibility to bake cookies on a random Tuesday and attend every gymnastics meet that your daughter competes in, or retiring early, or maybe you want to leave a career that feels like it's suffocating you, and what you really want is to make your own schedule and build your brand on your own terms.

Making your dreams happen begins with understanding what you truly want and how you want to feel.

As a real estate agent, I've witnessed firsthand how visualization can transform our lives. We watch our clients in real-time walk into a home and picture what their lives would look like if they woke up in that fixer-upper-turned-cozy-cottage, starter home, or luxury condo.

They're wondering, *How would it feel if this was my morning view while I drink my coffee? Will I feel safe and secure here? Will I feel like I upgraded my life? Do I picture my children running around in the backyard, chasing the puppy we'll get?* Being a real estate agent is so much bigger than selling homes and cashing your commission checks.

You have the power to transform your life into anything you want. You get to give yourself a permission slip to be completely happy, to become a millionaire, to stop worrying about money or not having enough time, to have every single part of your life feel wildly abundant.

But to do this, you need clarity. I want you to start by asking yourself two questions: "What do you actually want in your life?" and "How do you want to feel?"

I recommend you find somewhere quiet while you work through these questions. You can go for a walk, sit quietly at home, or go to your favorite coffee shop with a journal.

Getting clarity is not just about setting goals; it's about aligning your aspirations with your innermost values and emotions, ensuring that every step you take brings you closer to the life you've always dreamed of. We'll talk more about setting goals in the next section of the book, but let's focus on what you want your life to feel like first.

Start with visualization. *Write down everything you want and need to feel abundant.*

Here are some journaling questions to help you. As you write down the answers to these, remember—money and time are not obstacles. Don't worry about how to make this happen. For now, just visualize. Write down what your life would look like, if you were in the happiest, most abundant phase of your life.

Visualization Exercise

Where do you live? What does the house you want to live in look like? What does the neighborhood look like?

What's your morning routine? How do you want to feel every morning?

What does your day look like? What tasks do you do and which ones do you hand off to someone else?

Think about what kind of work you actually love to do and the things you do. List out your strengths as tasks you love to do, for example, "talking to clients" or "handling all the beautiful presentation details" and the tasks that drain you of energy as the type of work you want to outsource like "bookkeeping" or "managing my calendar."

What does your family look like? What do you spend extra money on to create comfort or special memories with your family?

This could include vacations, private school, classes or sports for your kids, a nanny, etc.

What do you invest money into that makes your life easier?

This could include things like housekeeping, a private chef or prepared meals, a personal trainer, driver, devices, grocery delivery, podcast or music subscriptions so you don't have to listen to ads, a second car, and/or an assistant.

What do you invest money in that makes you feel really good about yourself?

This could include things like spa days, getting your hair or nails done, clothing, a gym membership, meditation classes, therapy or personal development workshops, retreats, girls nights, etc.

What is your evening routine? How do you want to feel at the end of each day?

Building Your Dream Life

The next step is to actually take as many of these "dreams" and see what you can already accomplish now.

Maybe you can't hire a personal trainer immediately, but can you start going to a group exercise class with other women? *Probably.* And, while you're at it, you might just make a few connections who later become clients when they need to buy or sell a home.

Maybe you can take parts of your morning or evening routine and transform them instead of waiting. Maybe you can budget for a bookkeeper now if numbers and finances are not your thing.

Then, for the things you wrote down in your Visualization Exercise that you can't make happen yet, practice visualizing them every day. It is your job to keep your dreams front and center in your life. Put the list you wrote down on your wall where you can see it so it's always motivating you. Or, make a vision board if you're creative and want something more aesthetic.

You will need to hold onto this vision every time you lose a deal, you go a week without a single lead, a client ghosts you, or you hear, "We went with someone else." All of those things will happen at times; it is inevitable. They happened to me—and still do! It's all part of the real estate business. But the negative things and the low points do not have to define you.

Successful agent Tracy Tutor, known for her work on Million Dollar Listing, has often shared in interviews how she navigates the emotional rollercoaster of real estate. Her experience underscores the importance of resilience: "I have all these successes, and on the show, we're celebrated for selling luxury real estate at the highest level. All of those things are true, but for every 10 deals that I'm able to showcase on the show that were a success, or in some facet a success, there were 10 deals that I didn't get," she says. Even at the peak of her career, moments of self-doubt arise. "There are still those disappointments when I wake up and I say, 'God, what's it all for?'" she admits. Yet, she emphasizes, "You're gonna have those failures, and you have to embrace those too. They're part of the learning process."[2]

Estimates suggest that 75 percent of real estate agents leave the industry within the first year.[3] This statistic shouldn't discourage you; instead, use it as a reminder of the dedication and resilience required for long-term success.

You can become someone who closes millions in real estate deals each year. You can become a top agent. You can become the person in your network that people say "How the heck did she pull that off?" about.

It's not a question of success or failure. There's no such thing as failure if you're working toward your dreams; not in my book anyway. It's a question of success or quitting. And whether you succeed or quit is up to you.

Goal Setting

I recommend that you set goals for the year that truly shoot for the stars, but are also tangible and achievable! If you are a brand new agent, I would include several goals to get started and track your progress. These could look like:

1. Get my real estate license
2. Get my first homebuyer client
3. Close on my first deal
4. Close on five deals
5. Get my first seller client
6. Close $1 million in deals
7. Close $5 million in deals

If you already have some deals under your belt, review your numbers from last year and set goals that overwhelm but excite you. Your goals should feel a little scary!

Once you've written down all your goals, put them somewhere you can see them. It's also helpful to start saying your goals out loud. The more people who know about your goals, the more you'll be held accountable.

It's important to remember that not all goals have to be real estate-related. In addition to the real estate goals you just wrote down, I recommend you set other personal and professional goals. Whether it's fitness, relationships, finance, mental health, travel, self-improvement, or anything else, setting these goals will help you become a better person and a better agent. These goals should also be written down and prioritized in your schedule.

For example, one of my goals is to be more on top of my personal finances. As an agent, taxes are not automatically taken out of my commission checks, so I make sure to set aside 20–25 percent of each commission check in a separate account and forget about it until tax time. I also hired a real-estate-specific CPA to help me plan out the year and take advantage of write-offs and other tax benefits. No more surprise tax bills!

Download my free goal trackers at www.sheclosesdeals.com/trackers

Chapter 2
How to Choose a Brokerage

After you get your real estate license, you'll need to sign with a real estate brokerage. Picking the right one is a big decision. First, it's important to know that there are different types of real estate brokerages. The main types are Franchise Brokerages, Independent Brokerages, and Virtual Brokerages.

Franchise Brokerages

Think of them like: Familiar restaurant chains.

Pros: Strong brand recognition, established training programs, national network of colleagues.

Cons: Stricter policies, potentially higher fees, less flexibility in branding and marketing.

Examples: Keller Williams Realty, RE/MAX, Coldwell Banker.

Independent Brokerages

Think of them like: The local coffee shop where everyone knows your name.

Pros: Greater flexibility in branding and marketing, potentially higher commission splits, often offer a more personalized work environment.

Cons: May require more effort to build brand awareness, and might have fewer resources compared to larger franchises.

Examples: Sotheby's International Realty, The Agency, Compass.

Note: Some independent brokerages like Compass have national reach.

Virtual Brokerages

Think of them like: Online real estate offices.

Pros: Low overhead costs leading to potentially lower fees, ultimate flexibility in work location and schedule.

Cons: Limited access to in-person training and mentorship, requires strong self-motivation and marketing skills.

Examples: eXp Realty, Anywhere Advisors, Real Broker.

There's no "best" model, as the ideal choice depends on your individual needs and priorities. New agents might benefit from the structure and support of franchises, while experienced agents may prefer the flexibility of independent or virtual models.

Remember, choosing a brokerage is a two-way street. While they're assessing your potential as an agent, it's equally important for you to evaluate their offerings and culture. Researching different options, knowing your own priorities, and asking insightful questions during interviews will empower you to find the right fit for your career goals and personal development.

When you meet with a brokerage, don't be afraid to flip the script and interview *them!* Here are some questions you might ask them in the interview process.

Brokerage Interview Questions

Financial Considerations

- Commission structure:
  - What is the commission split for new and experienced agents?
  - Is there room for negotiation on the commission split? (This can often be renegotiated yearly, but not guaranteed.)
  - How is the commission split broken down? What portion does the agent receive, and what portion goes to the brokerage and other fees?
  - Do you have a cap when it comes to split?

- Fees:
  - What are your monthly fees, and what services are included?
  - Are there any additional or hidden fees I should be aware of?
  - Can you provide a breakdown of the fees associated with different services offered by the brokerage?

- Fee structures:
  - Does your brokerage offer alternative fee structures besides the traditional commission split, such as a flat fee or tiered system?
  - If so, can you explain how these alternative fee structures work and how they might benefit me?

Growth and Development

- Training and development:
  - How does your brokerage handle training and development costs?
  - Are there any financial contributions expected from the agent for training or development programs?
  - What resources and support does the brokerage offer for ongoing professional development?

- Mentorship options:
  - Do you offer mentorship programs for new agents?
  - How are mentors matched with new agents?
  - What level of support and guidance can I expect from a mentor?

Brokerage Culture and Environment

- How many agents do you have, and what is your agent retention rate?
- What is the company culture like?
- What's your involvement in the community?
- How many of your agents are full-time/part-time?
- What do you offer that other brokerages do not?
- What is the average income of your agents?

Interview with as many companies as you see fit, but I recommend a minimum of three. Tour the brokerage and ask to meet a few agents to hear about their experiences too.

Asking about company culture, community involvement, and meeting other agents can give you a sense of their values and whether you'd feel comfortable working there.

Your questions about the brokerage's goals, average income, mentorship options, and retention rate will give you a better idea of how challenged you will be and how much opportunity there is for you to grow.

Commission Split

When I first got into real estate my commission split with my brokerage was 55 percent and I had no idea that was low. While most brokerages keep their splits under wraps, industry talk usually puts new agent splits somewhere between 50 percent and 70 percent going to the agent. But here's the thing: just focusing on that number can be a rookie mistake.

Sure, a 70/30 split sounds great, but what are you really getting? Is the brokerage offering top-notch training, mentorship programs, and marketing tools to help you succeed? Or are you basically on your own?

You can also ask, "If I have a goal and hit it, are you able to increase my split?" There are many different ways to structure commission, but room for growth and openness for goal setting and conversation are most important.

The key takeaway? Don't just chase the highest split. Look for a brokerage that offers a fair split with room for growth, plus the support and resources you need to thrive as a new agent. You want to work with people who believe in you and invest in your success, not just their own bottom line.

Understanding Fees

In the beginning, the fewer fees your brokerage requires you to pay, the better. That's why sometimes it might be smarter to take a lower commission split without fees, than a higher commission split with fees, because as a new agent, you may not close a deal for several months, and you still have to pay the monthly fees regardless.

Typical fees include MLS quarterly fees, Realtor Dues, electronic signature platforms, CRM systems, and any marketing materials such as business cards, and can be a few hundred dollars a month. These fees can add up quickly, and you won't recoup any of that money until your first property closes.

Remember:

- **You can inquire about fee structures during interviews:** Ask each brokerage about the specific fees they charge and what each fee covers. This allows you to compare options and understand the total cost of doing business with each brokerage.

- **Consider the value proposition:** Fees aren't everything. Consider if the tools and resources offered can help you close deals and earn more, making the cost worthwhile.

Picking the Right Brokerage for You

Everyone is different, so what works for me might not work for you. My dislikes are low commission splits, restrictions on social media, and mandatory office hours. We had two agents join my brokerage from another company and they disclosed that their broker made them log their activities down to the hour each and every day. That would not work for me because I want to work independently.

I would recommend going with the brokerage where you feel the most at home and where you will be challenged and where you can see personal and professional growth rather than just being a number.

In the end, however, your brokerage does not determine your success. *You do.* They are not responsible for you doing well. *You are.*

After a few years in the business, I have learned that I could take my business anywhere and be successful. While having a supportive brokerage helps, it's ultimately your personal brand that drives your success. If you prioritize building your network and reputation, you'll continue to generate new leads regardless of which brokerage you're working for.

Chapter 3
My Three-Part Strategy to Become a Top Agent

My fast success in the real estate business comes down to these three things:

1. **Generating New Leads**

2. **Closing Deals**

3. **Referrals & Relationships**

Each part makes up 33 percent of a wheel that keeps spinning. There's not one single thing that will make you successful. It's the sum of all the small, daily actions that takes you to the top. You have to pay attention to your goals in all three areas to be successful, every single day. Throughout the remaining chapters of this book, I'll share exactly what I do to find success in each of these areas.

And there's one more part of becoming a top agent...

Become Confident in Yourself

You may not feel confident right now, but confidence can be built. I was not confident when I started, but I learned how to become confident over time and with practice.

As a real estate agent, you need to convey confidence and success in order to get potential clients to want to work with you.

The secret to confidence? *Consistency*.

You can become confident by doing things again and again. The first time, or even the first ten times you show a home, put in an offer, or negotiate a tough deal will feel challenging. But confidence can be built with time and practice.

Throughout this book, I share all of the strategies I learned to build up my confidence and become a top 1 percent agent. Remember, it took me almost six months just to pass the real estate exam. If I can do it, so can you.

Chapter 4
Generating New Leads

Top agents use a multi-faceted approach to generating new leads. My top two sources for leads are social media and my network, both of which are always sending me new potential clients and opportunities.

My Social Media Strategy

Social media has been one of my most effective strategies for attracting leads. There are two ways that social media helps me find new clients.

1. Attracting new clients by posting, commenting, and engaging constantly.

Example: *"Congrats to my buyers, Tom & Samantha (both tagged), on buying their first home! So happy we were able to get this done together!"*

It's likely that Tom, Samantha, and their family members will share this post, putting me and my brand in front of their entire network.

2. Supporting my professional network (lenders, agents, attorneys, etc.) by giving them public recognition.

Example: *"Another seamless transaction thanks to Dan (tagged) at [insert bank]. On to the next one!"*

Since I praised Dan in front of my entire network, he's likely to get more business. And since he's getting more business, he's likely to send me referrals. It's a win-win!

In order to pull off either of these strategies successfully, you need to be two things: authentic and consistent. People buy from real people and they love to know personal, interesting things about you. This is true for both your network partners, like lenders, and also true for your clients.

What to Post on Social Media

While sharing every second of your life isn't necessary, you'll get better results connecting with your audience by sharing personal details than you will by posting one *"Just Listed!"* graphic after another.

Lifestyle Content

Try to think about which parts of your life that make you "you." What do you tell people when they ask about who you are?

Lifestyle Content Ideas:

- Your workouts or favorite types of exercise
- Cooking or trying new restaurants
- Your engagement, wedding planning & wedding
- Travels & vacations
- Home decor projects
- Your favorite books or podcasts
- Mom life
- Walking your dog (dog-mom life)
- Where you volunteer

Once you've identified a few interesting things about yourself that you're comfortable sharing, this becomes part of your personal brand.

For example, if you love to try new restaurants, tag the places you go and share a little bit of content other foodies will love. Or, if you run half marathons, share those and share posts about training for races.

Write down two to three lifestyle-content ideas you can start sharing more of on social media.

_____
_____
_____

Share Your Wins

People are attracted to winners and success, which can feel frustrating when you're just starting out, and you don't have many clients or deals yet. You can learn to use this to your advantage, however, by making sure you get photos and videos of every client interaction you have.

Share every award you win, every new listing on the market, every home sold, every successful deal, every open house. Everyone should see your face. If you hold yourself back because you worry about annoying people, being cringe, or what people will think, you won't be very successful.

Your clients also need to see you out selling homes! Always be posting informal, behind-the-scenes content that shows people want to work with you.

Behind-the-Scenes Content Ideas:

- Signing up for your first real estate class
- Studying for your real estate license
- Getting your license
- Signing with your brokerage
- Happy clients at closing
- Clients signing paperwork
- Selfies with your just-listed homes or selfies with your clients
- You getting ready to go to showings

- Setting up at an open house
- Grabbing coffee before a busy day
- Take pictures and videos with your network partners and tag them on social!

Write down two wins you already have that you can share on social media this week.

_____

_____

_____

Consistency

Social media is a long game, and consistency is key. You won't get many leads from social media if you post a ton of content all in one day and then ghost your audience for two to three weeks. So, if this is not already a habit, schedule time in your calendar each week for creating social media content and also engaging with your audience.

You don't need to be on every single social media platform! You probably won't see many real estate leads or much success with social media if you try to post and engage on every single platform out there.

Pick one and spend most of your time posting and engaging there. I spend most of my time focused on Instagram, but I will repost content to other platforms like Facebook, LinkedIn, and TikTok.

If you already have a social media platform (ie., Instagram) that you enjoy using, and it aligns with your target audience, that's probably the best choice. It's easier to build on an existing habit than to start a new one. You can always add on other social media platforms or even hire a social media manager after you've expanded your business.

Response Time Matters

Your response time really matters. To be a top agent, you need to be available to your clients. If you don't respond to potential and current clients quickly, they will go elsewhere.

I usually respond within minutes, but a couple of hours *maximum*. If I took my time to respond, I would never do any deals! For real estate clients responses are expected to be immediate. No matter how busy you are, your clients are your business, and you have to make an effort to respond to messages as quickly as possible.

And for you introverts reading this, I hate to break it to you, but as an agent, you will have to talk on the phone. Different clients have different communication styles. If they like to talk, talk to them. If they like to text, text them. If they prefer email, email them.

Availability

Real estate requires nights and weekend work but you're in control of your schedule.

When it comes to showings, meetings, and open houses, you will have to find a balance between being able to move as quickly as possible to work with clients, and prioritizing your own needs for time off and family time.

Scheduling showings early in the mornings, evenings, and on the weekends is a strategy that Selling Sunset's Maya Vander uses to balance her clients' needs with her family. She says, "I really try to prioritize what's important, what I need to absolutely get done by like, 4:35 pm when my kids are back from school, and then obviously in real estate I have to do showings on the weekend, but I try to literally do it in like two hours so I could spend the rest of the day with the kids and do fun activities with them." This efficient approach can pay off in big ways. In Season 4, Episode 7 of Selling Sunset, Maya Vander demonstrates this by fitting showings around a busy client's schedule and caring for her newborn baby. Ultimately, she sold the property for $5.25 million within a month of listing.[1]

Chapter 5
Networking

I love the saying, "Your network is your net worth." The people closest to you will likely become your first clients. Many people get caught up with getting as many leads as possible, but if you are unable to land clients inside your circle, getting clients outside will be even harder. Start small, treat your first few clients like gold, and if you do a good enough job, it will eventually lead to more business.

As a new agent, many people in the real estate field will likely reach out to you to network and build a relationship. Say yes to every opportunity. But, have a plan.

It's easy to attend tons of agent-specific events and completely neglect to meet the other players in the industry (lenders, attorneys, etc.). This is a mistake I see many new agents make. They pour effort into their networking, but at the end of the day, they realize they've met dozens of other agents and not a single potential client or referral partner. Be sure you are putting your networking efforts toward building relationships that can help you close more deals.

Everyone feels awkward and has imposter syndrome when they start networking, but it's essential to building your team. It's kind of like being on a dating site. You won't vibe with everyone, but if you keep working at it, you will find your matches.

Ask good questions. If you're going to community events or meeting people for coffee, try using these questions:

- What is your story?
- How long have you been in the business?

- What made you get into this?
- What do you offer your clients that is different from other professionals?
- What are you looking for in a realtor/lender relationship?
- What are your short-term/long-term goals?
- How can I help you and your business?

Networking helps you generate new leads because it expands your list of contacts and people you can reach out to. As a new agent, learning to network can help you grow your business and your circle quickly. You never know who you might meet!

Chapter 6
Building Your Team

As an agent, you're only as good as the team around you. This is true at every level of business, including at the top. Selling Sunset's Emma Herman advises, "Find people you trust and who want the best for you and your business. Treat them with respect, compensate them for their hard work, and make sure you listen to the people around you."[2]

Whether it's your lender, landscaper, or anyone in between, you should be comfortable and confident connecting them with your clients. Having a strong team strengthens your personal brand and makes clients more likely to work with you in the future—and refer you to their network!

Lenders

Having more than one lender connection is helpful because some lenders specialize in certain types of financing. I have three lenders I work with regularly. I'm not against new relationships, but since I already have an incredible team of lending partners, I don't need to spend my time and energy searching elsewhere. Not only do they take care of my existing clients, but they also send me new leads regularly.

Attorneys

I may be a top agent with hundreds of deals under my belt, but I certainly don't know everything when it comes to legal matters. A knowledgeable attorney who's quick to respond is an important member of your team. Deals move fast, and you need someone who's just a quick phone call away to answer any questions or concerns, such as questions about titles or new construction.

Inspectors

Inspectors can make or break deals. In my experience, the best inspectors are straightforward, but not alarmists. You want someone who transparently tells your clients, "This is the problem, and this is what it would take to fix it," rather than scaring the client away from the deal.

Handymen

Handymen can come in handy on both sides of the transaction (see what I did there). On the sell side, a client may need to fix a few things before putting their house on the market. If you have a handyman readily available, you can save your client a lot of time and headaches, and make the listing process that much easier.

On the buy side, handymen are extremely valuable especially when the property needs repairs in order to meet the requirements of Federal Loan Financing (FHA or VA). You'll face one less objection when you can confidently say, "You have no need to worry as my handyman can take care of this!"

Cleaning Teams

A great cleaning team can make all the difference when it comes time to list a property. People don't want to buy a dirty house. Find a reliable and hard-working cleaning company that you can recommend to your sellers. I've even offered my cleaning team's services to my buyers as a closing gift!

Landscaping

Landscaping is the first thing a potential buyer sees when they pull up to the property. Curb appeal is everything! Having a reliable landscaper can also be handy for your buyers after they move in if they're planning on property repairs or small upgrades.

Photography / Videography

Photography and videography not only help you and your branding, but also assist in the exposure on the listing. You need to work with photo and video professionals. Don't do your clients a disservice by taking pictures from your cell phone.

Insurance

In many states, homeowner's insurance is a requirement. It may be cheaper for your client to bundle their home and car insurance if possible, but if not, it's great to have a trusted insurance agent to recommend.

Home Design / Staging

Staging a home can significantly boost its perceived value. Whether it's a seller looking to stage their home before listing, or a buyer looking to have their new home professionally furnished, having a connection to recommend for them will help you build your reputation.

Virtual staging is a great option as well. I had one client pay $125 for a virtual staging before listing their flip and the home was sold for $40,000 over the asking price. The more ways you can help your clients without spending too much of their money, the more they'll want to work with you in the future and refer you to their friends and family.

Where to Find Your Team

If you are a new agent, it can sometimes be difficult to find connections because more experienced professionals already have their established network connections and they're not looking to work with more people.

Here are some tips to help you connect with reliable professionals and build your dream team:

Leverage your existing network:

- Reach out to friends, family, and past colleagues. They might know reliable professionals they can recommend.

- Ask for connections from your real estate brokerage. Often, brokerages have established relationships with preferred vendors they can connect you with. Ask your broker or other agents in your brokerage for connections.

Search online:

- Professional association websites: Many professional associations, like the National Association of Realtors (NAR), offer member directories where you can search for qualified professionals in your area.

- Social media groups: Join local real estate groups on Facebook or search things like "real estate attorney Dallas" to connect with partners on social media.

Attend industry events:

I don't attend many events now that I have an established team and plenty of network referrals, but attending a lot of events was extremely helpful for making connections when I was just starting out.

- **Open houses and broker tours**: These events provide opportunities to meet various professionals in a casual setting and discuss potential collaborations.

- **Networking events**: Look for industry-specific networking events or workshops organized by local real estate associations or brokerages.

When you are new, you can also look for people who are also newly licensed or just starting their careers. Connections can last for a long time. Many of my strongest business relationships started when we were both new, and years later, we still refer business to each other.

Dream Team Checklist

Check off all the contacts you already have, and for the ones you don't, find two potential partners this week to schedule a coffee chat with. Even if you don't have your license yet, you can still grow your network and make connections now!

- Lender(s)
- Attorney(s)
- Inspector(s)
- Handyman
- Cleaning Teams
- Landscaper
- Photographer
- Videographer
- Homeowners Insurance
- Home Design/Staging

Chapter 7
Working with Buyers

Whether you're on the buy or sell side, you don't get paid until you close the deal. That's why understanding every part of the deal flow is so crucial, and why I'm going to share my exact playbook for getting deals done.

As an agent, you must address issues immediately as they arise. My experience has taught me that real estate isn't as seamless as it appears on Million Dollar Listing. I've found myself working until 2:00 AM, making unexpected two-hour drives, and arranging emergency repairs to close deals.

But going above and beyond for my clients is why I've been able to remain the top agent at my brokerage since I joined. These next sections in the book about working with clients are broken up into two parts: 1) working with buyers and 2) working with sellers. Let's do this.

Working with Buyers

As a new agent, it's likely your first buyers will be close friends and family. I became an agent when I was 25, and so I had a large pool of first-time home buyers in my personal network. I let everyone know that I was an agent and that I would take the best care of them if they worked with me.

As time went on, I made more connections, and more doors began to open. I kept in touch with everyone in my network and documented my journey into rental properties, Airbnbs, and co-management. This transparency attracted investors interested in similar strategies.

I didn't want to just *talk the talk*. I wanted to *walk the walk*. As a real estate investor myself, I was able to better showcase and explain the benefits of owning real estate (appreciation, cash flow, tax benefits, etc.) to my clients.

One client who found me on social media has bought 15 properties totaling $10,000,000+ thus far. You *never* know who is watching.

You might have just read this and thought, That seems impossible for me. Do you need to build a large portfolio of real estate investments yourself to establish credibility? Absolutely not. But it certainly helps. You can also become a top agent without buying a single property or even owning the home you live in. Start with the people you know, exceed their expectations, and you'll have a client for life. One client can quickly turn to five through word of mouth if you do a good enough job.

First Contact with Buyers

First impressions matter. When you're connecting with a new potential buyer, you need to convey confidence, excitement, and certainty that you're the right real estate agent for them. Your clients need to feel like you genuinely want to help them find and purchase a home.

Buyer's Questionnaire

Your Buyer's Questionnaire is the initial set of questions you ask someone when you first speak to them about becoming their real estate agent. These questions help you understand the client's needs and goals, and also helps define the parameters you'll need to set up in an MLS search (the database of homes and properties you'll have access to as a licensed agent).

By asking these questions upfront, I can create a personalized home search as soon as possible for my new prospective client. They're immediately impressed and the first part of their buying journey with me has begun.

When having my first conversation with buyers my script is always similar:

Step 1: Ask, "How have we connected?"

I always like to know where the lead or connection comes from. This helps me learn which social media channels or referral partners are sending me leads so I can continue to focus on them.

The next step is to build your client's excitement and ask some more clarifying questions.

Step 2: You can say something like: "Super exciting that you are getting ready to purchase a new home. You are in great hands with me and I will take care of you each step of the way. I do have a few questions to help get you started on your search."

From here, you can use your buyer's questionnaire. The full list of questions I ask is at the end of this book.

You can ask these questions via text, DM, email, or phone call. I prefer talking to my clients on the phone because I can ask them more details about something in the moment or ask how important something might be.

Buyer's Timeline

Finding out your potential client's timeline is also important. This will let you know if they are a hot, warm, or cold lead and how often you should contact them.

For example, if a potential client says they are ready to buy tomorrow, you can put more time into getting this client set up right away. If they're in no rush and "just thinking about it," you should still treat the client like a priority, but spend less time than you would on a hot lead.

Every buyer's timeline is different, which is why it's so important to have multiple clients in your pipeline. One of my first clients took over two years to purchase a home. Other clients fall in love with the first home they see.

It's not always apparent who's going to purchase quickly and who might drag their feet. Sometimes you need to trust your intuition and adjust your priorities accordingly.

Always Get a Preapproval

A preapproval is an estimated maximum budget a lender sets for your client after reviewing their financial health (work history, income, savings, assets, and credit). A preapproval is also helpful for not wasting your time on clients who aren't ready to buy! Once a client gets preapproved, you know they are serious.

You should *never* take clients out to see homes without a preapproval letter from their lender or take clients to see homes that exceed their preapproval budget. The last thing you want is to show your client a home they can't afford since it will frustrate and disappoint them.

Make Sure They Know You're Their Agent

It's important to have a written agreement with your buyers so that they are aware of your commission. Also, with a written, exclusive buyer's agreement in place, the client cannot have another agent show them any homes or represent them during the time the agreement is in place.

Early in my career, one of my clients went to an open house and put an offer in with the listing agent and I lost out on the deal! I did not have a buyer's agreement, and I did not communicate well enough to my clients that if they wanted to put in an offer, they'd need to contact me after the showing. Now, if my clients are going to open houses, I instruct them to call me afterward if they love the home. If you do not teach your clients this, they won't know!

Be a Confident Guide for Your Clients

Some of your clients may want to go see every single home on the market or feel like they know the market better than you.

As a real estate professional, you're the expert in navigating the market for your clients. Confidence in your knowledge and abilities is key to building trust.

Here are some strategies to cultivate confidence:

- **Know the Market:** Stay up to date on market trends, property values, and neighborhood nuances. The more you know, the more confident you'll be guiding clients toward informed decisions.
- **Realistic Expectations:** Set realistic expectations for your clients regarding purchase price, interest rates, terms, and other details during their property search.

- **Creative Problem Solving:** Don't just help your clients identify problems—figure out how to solve their problems in creative ways. The more you can showcase your knowledge through action, the more your client will trust you.

Overdeliver for your Clients

Challenge yourself to become the best real estate agent you can be. For me, this means checking the MLS & Realtor.com three times per day and sending my clients any homes that match their search criteria if I see something new.

Sure, clients will get this info in an automated email from the MLS search we set up, but when I show them that I am prioritizing them by sending them any new homes personally with a text or email, I'm setting myself apart from other agents.

Going the extra mile is key to exceeding client expectations. Even something as small as treating them to coffee before meeting up for a showing can go a long way. I usually say something like: "I'm stopping at Starbucks. Would you like a coffee before our appointment? My treat!" Coffee is the love language of many people, and this is a quick and easy way to stand out and build a relationship with your client.

Listen to Your Client's Needs

The lender preapproval shows the maximum amount a house a client can afford, but that amount might be out of their financial comfort zone. Before house hunting, discuss their ideal monthly payment to find the "sweet spot" that feels manageable. This ensures that everyone's on the same page and can save you a lot of potential time and headache.

Remember, happy clients lead to happy recommendations! The goal is to find a home they love, not just one they can technically afford.

Samantha DiBianchi from Million Dollar Listings often says that listening to clients is what helps her close deals. For example, if a client says, "Well I don't like the kitchen," she won't just say "Okay let's move on to the next house." She will ask, "What don't you like about the kitchen?" or "What are you looking for?" to fully understand what her clients are looking for or what they're thinking at that particular moment.[1]

Put in Offers as Soon as Possible

When your clients are ready to make an offer, time is always of the essence. The sooner you can send in your client's offer, the better. It's always better to over-communicate during the offer stage. Don't leave people guessing. If I know I will be on the road all day, driving from showing to showing, and I can't write an offer up until later that night, I will text the seller's agent and let them know that an offer is coming in.

The sooner the seller is aware of your offer, the greater chance your client has of winning the deal.

How to Write a Great Offer

Once your clients have found their perfect property, it's your job to help them put in the best offer possible. Before this point, you should already have researched the market so you know what a competitive offer will be. Recent sales of comparable properties and current market trends will guide you in formulating a competitive price.

It's also important to analyze the seller's situation. Are they motivated for a quick sale, or willing to wait for a higher price? You don't know this unless you talk with the seller's agent, so I always put in a call to them prior to my client submitting an offer to see if there is anything specific their clients are looking for. This knowledge empowers you to make a strategic bid.

Finally, don't just focus on price. Package your offer with factors that make your client an attractive buyer. Are your clients preapproved for a mortgage, demonstrating financial readiness? Can you offer a flexible closing date that aligns with the seller's needs? Emphasize these strengths to make your offer stand out.

At the end of this book, you will find my scripts for texts and emails I send to the seller's agent highlighting the strengths of my clients' offers!

Under Contract

Getting an offer accepted is exciting! Your job isn't done though. Now you've got to see the deal all the way to the closing table.

Immediately Advise Your Buyers of the Next Steps

It's important to educate your buyers on the "do's and don'ts" while they are under contract.

When I was a new agent, a client co-signed for her boyfriend's new car two days before closing and we weren't able to close on the home. It turns out co-signing a car loan (or any kind of loan) can mess with mortgages. Now, I share this story with new agents to remind them to chat with their buyers about their finances (especially once a deal is under contract).

Buyers should not:

- Quit their job

- Deposit or extract large chunks of money that can not be traced

- Take on new debt such as buying a car, furniture, or a vacation

- Open a new credit card

- Close any financial accounts

- Miss or skip any monthly payments

The general rule of thumb is that buyers should avoid any changes in their personal finances if possible once their offer has been accepted.

Gather & Send All Necessary Documents

Your buyer's lender will be requesting a lot of documentation. It's your client's responsibility to get these documents sent over to the lender, but it's your job to make sure they are doing this as quickly as possible. During this time, you will be sending weekly texts or phone calls to your clients (my scripts for these can be found at the end of this book) to make sure they are on track. You should also be checking in with the lender to make sure everything is running smoothly.

Inspection Period

Most clients go into an inspection thinking it's going to make or break the deal. While inspections are important to identify potential issues, it's more of a neutral report about the home itself, not a "yes/no" for the deal.

I always tell my clients they will get a PDF version of the inspection that they can keep as a to-do list and tackle as needed over the next few months or years. It's also important to know you will *never* receive a flawless inspection. Even new-construction homes have issues!

I recommend working with inspectors who are straightforward, but not alarmists. This is why having a team you can trust is so important. You want to work with inspectors who guide and educate your clients during the home inspection.

Types of Inspections

I always recommend the big four: general inspection, termite inspection, radon test, and water check. At the end of the day, however, your client is in charge of which inspections they want done. Your main goal is for your client to be comfortable with the purchase and feel fully informed about the condition of the house.

You also might have specific inspection types required by your state, so check with your brokerage if you're not sure what is required by law.

Final Walkthroughs

The final walkthrough will take place the night before or morning of closing. This is when you go around the house making sure it's still standing (you'd be surprised), and in the condition you were expecting.

As the agent, you'll walk through the home with your client and check the following:

- Make sure appliances are still there (if part of the sale)
- Run all faucets, toilets, showers, and dishwashers to check for leaks
- See that nothing has been damaged or modified in the home

I once did a final walkthrough and found three feet of water standing in the basement. Luckily, we were able to get an extra $3,500 off the price on the spot because of it. That's the magic of the final walkthrough—sometimes you have to deal with surprises, but you can also snag some serious wins for your clients!

You also want to have details for your clients about what to expect at closing, what documents to bring, and what utilities they will need to transfer over.

The final walkthrough is also a great opportunity to take pictures of your clients holding your personalized "sold" sign and even get a selfie with them! This is a great way to showcase your happy clients and remind people that you're a serious agent who closes deals.

Chapter 8
Working with Sellers

Now that we've covered everything you need to know to start working with home buyers, it's time to talk about my favorite type of client: sellers! I prefer working with sellers because I have more control when it comes to commissions, listing prices, and negotiating offers.

Commissions

As an experienced seller's agent, I charge a 4 percent commission to my sellers. It takes time and experience to be able to charge a premium commission; I certainly didn't start out that way! I started out charging 2 percent, and now I don't offer anything under 4 percent as the listing agent unless I'm working with family, friends, or a repeat client.

The changes to commission structure that we discussed at the beginning of this book only apply to your commission when you represent the buyer. Seller's agent commissions remain the same.

I think new agents should consider offering 2 percent until they have a few deals closed. This is a great way to try to beat out other agents who (like me) are asking for a 4 percent commission. Standard commissions might vary by brokerage and location, so talk with your broker and other agents to get a sense of what is typical in your area.

How to Get Listings

There are lots of different ways to get listings. For me, it's networking.

Your Own Network

Many of your seller clients should be coming to you naturally through your network. They might find you through a referral from a past client, or social media, or at a networking event.

I've talked about this already, but you should start by focusing on your "circle." My past clients and network partners are always mentioning my name and referring me to new clients. If you are trying to get more listings, pay attention to growing your network first.

You can also use additional strategies below to help you find listings. These are things I do from time to time, but they don't send me as many clients as my own network and social media.

Farming Neighborhoods

Real estate farming is a marketing strategy where you choose specific neighborhoods to become known as *the* go-to real estate agent for that area and send mailers, letters, and leave goodie bags multiple times per year.

Lots of agents focus on their local neighborhoods, which is smart, but I like to double down and do the same for areas where I have listings. There's always a buzz in the neighborhood when a house sells! People are interested in the sale price, and it can make them wonder what their own home might be worth.

Even if you're a brand new agent and you don't have any sales yet, you can pull up recent closings on the MLS and create flyers that say "123 Main Street just sold for record-breaking pricing of X [amount]! Yours can be next."

I recommend starting with two to three neighborhoods. Be a familiar face! People remember who they see regularly. Some agents try to be everywhere at once, but it's better to build strong connections in a few areas than have a scattered presence everywhere.

When it comes to mailers, flyers, and even social media graphics, there are so many templates to choose from in Canva for free. Or if you want to go the more done-for-you route, there are direct mail websites that will handle almost everything for you. No matter what your budget is, there are ways to make this strategy work.

Expired Listings

Another way to capture leads is through expired listings. In the MLS, pull up all expired listings and "skip trace" the owner's phone number. Skiptracing is the process of tracking down an individual's information such as phone number, email, or home address.

With expired listings specifically, contacting the owner of a property can potentially reignite their interest in selling their property. You could win them over by recommending new marketing or pricing strategies, or by proving how you can outperform their current agent. You'd be surprised at how many new listings you can get from this strategy!

It's important to note that there are legal and ethical guidelines to follow when it comes to finding client's information and contacting them, and it's crucial to ensure you are complying with all applicable laws and regulations.

Listing Appointments

Once someone agrees to talk to you about selling their home, it's time to make a listing appointment to see the home and talk to the seller in person! When it comes to setting up a new listing, I use the same strategy every time.

Once entering the client's home, I let them give me a tour of their home. It's their house, and I let them drive completely. This tour is all about highlighting *their* property. I make clients feel like rockstars and point out all the things I love about their homes.

Don't say anything negative or point out things that need to be improved at this initial appointment (that comes only later once the paperwork is signed). You need to be positive and kind. You are creating a relationship the minute you walk in the door. Use this tour as time to listen more than talk.

After the tour, I ask the seller to sit down and we go through a list of questions to make sure I have all the details of the home. Then, I start my "why me" pitch.

Know Why Clients Should Choose You

Your sellers will likely be interviewing other agents to represent their house. Not only do you need to know how to sell a home, but you also need to know how to sell yourself. What makes you better than the competition?

Your confidence when you pitch yourself to your potential clients has to be high. I learned this the hard way when I sat down for my first listing appointment. The client said, "Why should we hire you?" and I didn't have an answer prepared. Because I didn't know what to say, I did not come across as confident in my ability to sell the home. As you might have guessed, I didn't get the listing.

I learned my lesson quickly after that! The "why me" pitch is important because it shows your selling ability even before you get the deal, and gives you a chance to impress your potential client.

Practice your speech and then practice it ten times more than you think you need to. I have given my "why me" speech so many times that I can now do it in my sleep. The more listing appointments you get, the more you'll be able to give your "why me" pitch confidently.

You don't need an extensive track record to prove to your clients that you're the right fit. New agents can share the credibility and track record of the brokerage they work for—such as homes sold, sale prices, and other relevant information.

You can also win clients over by showcasing your knowledge of the neighborhood. If you do your research and know the market and the area better than any other agent, you can prove that you're the right agent to list their property, regardless of your sales history.

Jade Mills, an agent who has closed deals with celebrity clients like Byron Allen, Kim Kardashian, and Cindy Crawford, says, "Knowledge is the most important thing in our business. You must know everything about every property you sell and be the most knowledgeable agent when you go on a listing appointment."[1]

Amen! Know the house better than the owners do and you'll immediately gain credibility.

Another way to differentiate yourself is to offer 24/7 open communication. Tell your clients, *"You will be working with me and me only,"* which is a big deal for sellers who've dealt with frustrating hand-offs at large brokerages.

Comparative Market Analysis (CMA)

After selling myself in the "why me" pitch, I move on to the next step, which is everyone's favorite part: money! I love being able to tell the client how much I think we can sell their house for based on my CMAs. A CMA estimates a property's value by comparing it to similar recently sold homes in the area.

I always complete my CMA prior to going to a client's house because I want to be fully prepared before meeting. I also consider what Zillow shows, because even though it's not always perfect, it's where many sellers check first. This helps me tailor my approach and understand where the client's expectations might be.

Then through the MLS system, I look for comparable properties that have sold within 12 months with similar beds/baths/square footage near the subject property and generate the CMA. I typically list three to five of the most relevant comps to include in the analysis.

Side note: Zillow has actually been sued more than once for giving inaccurate Zestimates.[2] Third-party sites are fine to get an initial feel for a property's value, but any further digging should be done on the MLS. This is where you'll find disclosures and remarks for the listing as well.

You've Got the Deal

Once you've mastered the "why me" pitch and secured your first client, it's time to get to work!

As the real estate agent, you're in charge of preparing your client's home for sale and directing your client on everything they can do to help present the home in the best way possible. This all starts with the pre-sale inspection.

Pre-Sale Inspection

Prior to going on the market, I like to do what I call a pre-sale inspection. It's basically me putting on my inspector hat and going through the entire house giving my professional, honest opinion—after the listing paperwork is signed.

Here's everything you should go through during your pre-sale inspection before listing the home on the market.

1. Declutter

Decluttering and/or getting a storage unit is almost always needed. Less is always more and makes all spaces look bigger. As a general rule, there should be nothing on the counters in the kitchen or bathrooms and nothing on refrigerators such as magnets or photos. Even small details like organizing all the hangers in the closet can make a difference, so be as thorough as possible!

2. Depersonalize

The goal is for buyers to come into the house and visualize it as their own, not as someone else's home. This means your client will need to depersonalize every room. Depersonalizing includes taking down pictures and removing very personal decor like trophies, signs, and things made by their kids.

3. Touch-ups

Your clients should touch up paint or fix minor bumps and scratches on walls, doors, and cabinets. Normal wear and tear happens, and sometimes it can blend into the background for homeowners.

Since you can see the home with fresh eyes, it's important to look for these and make a list with your client to get these things repaired.

4. Deep Cleaning

Have a professional team clean the home prior to going on the market. This is a worthwhile investment. Potential buyers may not even notice how clean the house is, but they will certainly notice a dirty house.

Sometimes, I even throw in a free cleaning as part of my package—it doesn't cost much for me and it's one less thing for the client to worry about.

5. Home Aromas

Smell plays a major factor in the sale of a house.[3] Make sure to bring a new candle, wax melt, or diffuser prior to going on the market. Citrus, vanilla, and freshly baked bread or cookies are the best scents to use in my opinion.

If a house smells like pets or smoke, it will be a turn off, but a house smelling like freshly baked cookies or clean linens can sway a potential buyer.

6. Small Touches

In addition to making the home smell great, I also provide a fresh bouquet of flowers and a welcome mat. Small touches make a difference!

7. Exterior Maintenance

The exterior of the home is the first thing a potential buyer sees. Direct your clients to pull weeds, put down new mulch in the flowerbeds, power wash the home, and have freshly cut grass to enhance the curb appeal.

The more of these pre-sale inspection changes you can handle for your client, the better. It shows you're a pro who anticipates needs, and they'll love having one less thing to worry about. If the cost of these things is relatively small, I often pay for these as part of the "cost of doing business." If it's a larger ticket item like exterior maintenance, the client will pay, but I will help connect them to someone who can provide the service.

Preparation to Listing Timeline

Once the house is prepared, it's time to schedule photography and videography, and get the property listed on the market.

My timeline to listing a property typically looks like this:

Thursday / Friday: Pre-sale inspection walkthrough with sellers.

Monday: Cleaning and landscaping.

Tuesday: Pictures and videos.

Wednesday: Going on the market.

Wednesdays are my magic days to hit the market with showings starting immediately.

Thursday: Private showings.

Friday: Private showings and open house.

Saturday: Private showings and open house.

Sunday: Private showings and open house.

Of course, this timeline varies if there are repairs that need to be made or work to be done before the property is ready to be put on the market.

Finding a Buyer in the First Week

The first week the home is on the market is the most important time to set the stage and get the best offer.

The longer the house sits on the market, the less likely it is that your listing will get offers at or above the asking price. So, the minute the home goes on the market, it's your job to get the most amount of exposure possible.

You want to post your new listing on all your social media platforms, in any relevant online groups, and to your current email database.

Where to market your new listing:

- Local Facebook groups
- Your own social media profiles
- Your broker's social media profiles
- Your social media stories
- In "just listed" emails to your network
- To buyer's agents on the MLS

As you start to build a following, you might already have interested buyers for a new listing within your existing network. This is fantastic because if you are the agent of both the buyer and the seller in a double-ended deal, you earn the entire commission! If you rely only on the MLS to sell your client's home, you don't have much of a chance to double dip.

These types of deals can be very challenging, but rewarding. Recently, I double-ended a 1.75 million-dollar transaction where negotiations were particularly intense. And even though that transaction probably took a few days off of my life, I learned a lot and we did eventually make it to the closing table.

It's very important that if you do have a double-ended transaction that you are transparent and honest with your clients on both sides about the deal. Not all states allow agents to work double-ended deals, and some require specific written disclosures, so check your state laws as well.

Open Houses

Open houses are a great way to get the maximum amount of eyeballs on your listing in the shortest amount of time. I like to hold three open houses over the first weekend that the house is on the market to (hopefully) be under agreement by the following Monday.

Like I mentioned before, the first week a house is on the market is the most important!

My typical open-house timeline is:

- Friday night 5:30 pm - 7:30 pm
- Saturday 11:00 am - 1:00 pm
- Sunday 11:00 am - 1:00 pm

If I have multiple open houses in a weekend, I will plan 10:00 am–12:00 pm for House #1 and 2:00–4:00 pm for House #2, and alternate time slots each day so each property gets to experience each time frame.

With two different properties, for example, I would do:

Friday
House #1 2:00 pm - 4:00 pm
House #2 5:30 pm - 7:30 pm

Saturday
House #1 10:00 am - 12:00 pm
House #2 2:00 pm - 4:00 pm

Sunday
House #2 10:00 am - 12:00 pm
House #1 2:00 pm - 4:00 pm

In my experience, the 11:00 am–1:00 pm time frame is the most successful, but this could also vary depending on your target audience and geographical area. After a few open houses, take notes on which time frames have the largest number of attendees.

Open houses help my business in multiple ways. I have the opportunity to secure a buyer for my seller clients, I can find new potential clients looking to buy a home if this particular property doesn't work out, and it's an opportunity for me to get photos and videos for my personal brand as a real estate agent.

I always work to make sure my open houses always have the right vibes. A warm inviting atmosphere always helps buyers envision the house as a home! This is why I *always* include live, acoustic music at open houses for my homes over $500,000.

Even if you don't want to go this far, you can also help create the right environment with inexpensive extras like a candle or fresh flowers.

Open houses are also a great way to potentially double-end a deal (if done correctly). You should always have open house sign-in sheets that have all buyers write their name, phone number, email address and check off if they are working with an agent or not. This way, if an open house attendee isn't working with an agent, you can possibly represent them as the buyer as well.

Whenever possible, try to avoid hosting open houses with other agents. For safety reasons, you can have someone else there, but I recommend you have one of your lenders, attorneys, or similar network partners host with you instead of another agent.

Once, I held an open house at an adorable home and had two new agents with me. A cash buyer walked in the door and said he wanted to put an offer in *that* day. There we were, the three of us, drooling at this offer!

If it had just been me there, I would have easily double-ended the deal, made a new connection and called it a day. But since there were two other agents with me, I had the three of us do rock, paper, scissors (a wild but true story) to represent the buyer and unfortunately, my scissors lost me the deal and I was forced to split the commission with one of them.

Your open houses should always have:

- The MLS listing sheets
- Your business cards

- The open house sign-in sheet
- A feedback sheet
- Fresh flowers
- A great-smelling candle

Private Showings

Private showings are when other agents are showing your client's home to their potential buyers outside of an open house. Try to attend as many of these as you can!

Even though you aren't the agent leading the showing, you can answer any questions that might come up from the buyer and highlight all the amazing features of the home.

You should also arrive early and do a walkthrough of the home to make sure everything looks the way it should before the showing. This is another way to be a stand-out agent and build a professional relationship with your agent colleagues by going above and beyond for their buyers.

Presenting Offers to Your Clients

It's so exciting when your client has offers rolling in! Present the offers to your seller as the offers come in to keep them in the loop and respond quickly to any potential opportunities.

Offer details to share with your clients:

- Purchase price
- Deposits
- Offer expiration
- P&S date
- Closing date
- Mortgage type and what percentage down payment

- Inspection period
- Any additional terms like appliances staying or contingencies

Also, remember not to give your personal opinion on any offers until all potential offers are in. Stay as objective as possible.

Make sure to keep your clients informed about the process though and that the first offer is not always the final offer. Clients often get excited and start to feel pressured to make a decision immediately, but if you expect multiple offers, encourage your clients to wait on their decision until more offers are in.

Negotiating the Deal

Once all of the offers are on the table, it's time to go to work.

My favorite part of this process is seeing how much higher and better I can negotiate offer terms for my clients. If you have multiple offers on the table, make sure the buyers are aware of one another. I typically call all of the buyers' agents and ask for the highest and best offers. I say to buyers agents, "We are reviewing all offers. If your client would like to submit a new highest and best offer please let me know by X date and time."

You can also say *"Look, my client really likes your offer and there is another offer very similar. If you can come up to $X the property is yours."* Inviting multiple buyers to compete for the same property can sometimes increase the offers for your clients.

Handling Low-Ball Offers

Negotiating offers is an art form in real estate, and lowball offers are a reality you'll likely face. According to a report by the National Association of Realtors (NAR), 84 percent of sellers reported receiving at least one offer below asking price.[4] It's important to stay calm, professional, and prepared to counter effectively. It's important to stay calm, professional, and prepared to counter effectively.

While lowball offers can be frustrating, remember:

- **Buyers are Negotiating:** In competitive markets, you might have multiple offers over asking price, but it's also common for buyers to start with a lower offer, leaving room for negotiation.

- **Be Prepared:** Do your research on recent sales of comparable properties in the area (comps) to understand the property's true market value. This will be your ammunition when countering a lowball offer.

Staying prepared and highlighting the property's value can still lead to a successful outcome.

Get Your Offers Under Signed Contract as Soon as Possible

Once your client has settled on an offer and is ready to accept, you want to get the offer signed ASAP. A verbal offer means almost nothing. Also, do not inform any of the buyers' agents that their offer was not accepted until you have a signed offer in your inbox from your top offer.

If your top offer does not go through for whatever reason, you want to be able to move on to the other offers if possible.

After the Contract is Signed

Politely follow up with all the offers your client didn't accept. Contact the buyer's agents and thank them for their offers and if anything changes that they'll be the first to know.

Here is what I say to the buyer's agents whose offers were not accepted: "Thank you very much for your offer and if anything happens, I will gladly let you know. I hope our paths cross again in the future."

If there were multiple offers on the table, I sometimes like to add to the message, "There were X amount of offers on the table," just so the buyer's agent is able to go back and relay this information to their clients.

It's generally understood among agents that you do not disclose specific offer amounts and terms. Remember, a good reputation is important and you want buyer's agents to want to work with you.

Inspections

After the offer is accepted by your clients, the buyers enter their inspection period. Buyers can pull out of the offer any time for any reason during this period. There is also a clause in some states' laws that gives buyers until 5:00 pm on the day *following* the inspection period to back out for any reason. Verify that you are aware of your state and local laws regarding inspection periods.

From the seller's perspective, the shorter the inspection period, the better, since it gives less time for the buyers to back out. Nothing is worse than having buyers wait until the last day of the inspection period to back out.

Inspections can make or break a deal. As a seller's agent, I want to try and do everything I can to offer solutions to problems that come up during the inspection.

This is another reason why your network partners are *so* important. If issues come up during the inspection, I can advise the buyer's agent to ask for necessary repairs to be made to keep the deal from falling through. I then share my network partners (handyman, landscaper, electrician, etc.) with my seller to complete the repairs.

If all else fails, I'll talk to my clients and the buyer's agent and open up the conversation for a reduced purchase price or a credit at closing for the buyers to take care of the repairs.

Appraisals

Cash offers will always be king, however, if your seller accepted an offer that has bank financing, appraisals become an extremely important part of the deal. An appraisal is a professional assessment of a property's fair market value, considering factors like size, condition, location, and recent sales of similar homes. It's part of your job as the seller's agent to help the property appraise. I attend all appraisals and answer any questions the appraiser might have about the property.

Attending the appraisal also gives you the chance to build a positive relationship with the appraiser. I am always friendly with the appraiser and try to make small talk. I ask where the appraiser is from, how long they've been in the industry, and if they have cards that I can pass out to clients since I'm always looking for a great appraiser to refer clients to.

I thank them for coming out and make sure they call me if they have any additional questions. Being nice goes a long way!

If you want to go the extra mile, come prepared to the appraisal with comparables in hand that are at or above the property's purchase price. Appraisers are busy people and may not have the same amount of time that you do to focus on your client's property. Make it easy for them.

If an offer comes in that seems significantly above market value, there's a good chance that it won't appraise, no matter how great the appraiser is. It's important to communicate this clearly to your client and what this means for the offer.

In one case, my client received an offer $75,000 over asking price. Knowing it likely wouldn't appraise, we ultimately decided to accept a cash offer that was $20,000 lower. As I mentioned before, cash is king.

P & S, Walkthrough, & Closing

The Purchase & Sale Agreement is the "blueprint" of the real estate deal. It's essentially the roadmap for the entire transaction, ensuring both buyer and seller are on the same page. This comprehensive document outlines the rights, responsibilities, and contingencies for both buyer and seller, serving as a crucial safeguard throughout the closing process.

Purchase & Sale ("P&S")

While the initial offer establishes a foundation, the P&S dives much deeper. It details a range of critical aspects, including:

- **Inspections and Disclosures:** The P&S outlines the timeframe for inspections (home, pest, etc.) and lays out what needs to be disclosed by the seller about the property's condition.

- **Financing Deadlines:** The P&S sets clear deadlines for securing financing, ensuring both parties understand the timeline for the buyer's mortgage approval.

- **Closing Costs:** The agreement breaks down the closing costs for both buyer and seller, leaving no room for surprises at the final table.

- **Contingency Clauses:** These clauses address what happens if unforeseen circumstances arise, such as issues found during inspections, appraisal shortfalls, or inability to secure financing.

- **Title and Deed:** The P&S specifies how the title will be transferred and the type of deed used, ensuring a clean and secure transaction for the buyer.

While the P&S is a detailed document, it's also not uncommon for questions or clarifications to arise. As the seller's agent, your role is to guide your clients through the intricacies of the agreement. Take time to explain each section of the agreement to your clients in a clear and concise manner, or refer them to their attorney if it's something they need legal advice on.

For any specific questions about the deal though, it's always a good idea for clients to have their attorney take a look. That's what attorneys do best. Remind your client that even though they might not be writing a check directly, the attorneys are getting paid from the deal and should be consulted regularly.

You may also need to do more negotiating on behalf of your clients when finalizing the P&S. While the P&S is a standard form, there's always room for negotiation on specific terms like closing dates, repair requests, or inclusions. Advocate for your clients' best interests during this crucial stage.

Your main job during this stage, however, is to frequently touch base with all relevant parties—your clients, the buyer's agents, lenders, and the attorneys—as needed to make sure that everything stays on track. I keep track of the P&S date for all my deals to make sure the attorneys have everything ready to meet the deadline. At the end of this book, you'll find the weekly text updates I send to buyers and sellers throughout the closing timeline, depending on which side of the deal I am working.

Final Walkthrough

The final walkthrough is when the buyer and their agent have an opportunity to walk the property and inspect that everything is in the condition they agreed to when they put in their offer on the home.

As the seller's agent on the morning of the buyer's final walkthrough, it's a good idea to go walk the property to ensure everything is out of the house and that it's left in broom swept condition. This will give you and your client peace of mind before heading to the closing table.

Closing

Closing day is an exciting time for your client, and for you, of course! Be sure to keep your client up to date throughout the entire day and notify them immediately of any action items that might come up. I always text my clients first thing in the morning with a "Happy closing day!!!"

Don't forget to take pictures and tag your clients and your team on your social media, congratulating everyone on a successful deal.

Closing Gifts

At this point, you've done everything you can to overdeliver for your client, so why not impress them one last time with a closing gift? After closing, drop off or mail your sellers a gift and thank them for trusting you in the process.

Closing gifts I've sent in the past include a fresh bouquet of flowers in a vase, a "welcome" basket with essentials, and a $100–$250 gift card to HomeGoods or Lowes. It all depends on the client and the property. Another idea is to send a bottle of champagne or confetti that clients can pop for a video. This is great for social media!

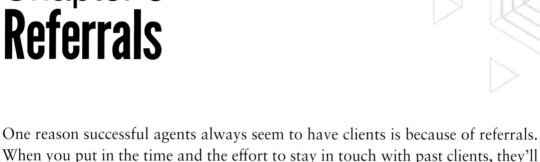

Chapter 9
Referrals

One reason successful agents always seem to have clients is because of referrals. When you put in the time and the effort to stay in touch with past clients, they'll refer new clients to you if you exceeded their expectations before.

This is why I put so much emphasis on relationship-building and gaining referrals. There are a few ways beyond check-in texts and tagging people on social media that I leverage my past clients and network partners for referrals. Let's go deeper!

Getting Client Reviews

People want to see proof that you have helped other clients similar to them, so they can feel confident that you'll be able to help them too.

Reviews are one of the best ways to offer your potential clients proof of your work. You should work on building a collection of reviews on social media, Google, and your website for future clients to browse through.

Ask your clients for Facebook or Google reviews after every closing. So many agents neglect to do this. I typically wait until one week after closing to request a review, and then remind them two or three times afterward. Your clients are often busy after the closing, so if you don't remind them, they will forget too, even though they likely want to leave you a positive review.

Request Reviews

If you've already sold a few homes but haven't gotten reviews yet, make a list of every client you need to reach out to to request reviews. Text them now using the exact message I send to clients.

Write down three Past Clients you can ask for a review

_____

_____

_____

Download my texting templates at sheclosesdeals.com/scripts!

Staying in Touch with Past Clients

Just because you've closed the deal doesn't mean your work is done. Not only can past clients refer you to their network, but they might also become repeat clients themselves. The average homeowner moves every 7 years, sometimes even sooner, creating new opportunities to help them find their dream home (again!).

You never know when someone might need an agent. The more people who think of your name when someone says "real estate agent," the better. Every top agent has a circle of influence with past clients, social media, and network partners that constantly feed them new business.

Every quarter, I text everyone in my phone contacts offering "discounts" or gift cards if they buy, sell, or refer a client within that quarter. People love free stuff and being rewarded, so I always try to incentivize new business with this strategy!

Treating Your People like Gold

Take care of your people and prioritize the contacts and partners you have.

Every industry relationship you have is a two-way street. You don't want to send other people clients with no reciprocation on their end. Similarly, if a network partner is sending you leads and getting nothing in return, they'll likely stop.

Once I develop a strong relationship with a partner, I let them *know* that they're one of my go-tos. Since my clients generally only need one of these partners in a specific category (lender, attorney, handyman, etc.), I keep my circle somewhat small.

For example, I work with three specific lenders that I know I can trust to do good work, and I don't generally recommend anyone else. Even though my clients can choose a different lender, these partners know that I'm referring them to every single client of mine in need of a lender.

My first lender relationship actually started with my very first real estate deal. I had absolutely no idea what I was doing. My client had no clue that they were my first client! So I called my client's lender and I told her, "This is my first deal, the client doesn't know, literally nobody knows and I have no idea what I'm doing." So she took my hand and walked me through the entire process.

To this day, she's one of the few lenders I refer clients to, and she sends me referrals as well. All because she took me under her wing and helped a new agent who was struggling.

One more thing—don't forget about tagging and interacting with your network partners on social media! People love to get recognized in public, and something that takes you 30 seconds can help to build a lasting relationship.

Relationships with Other Real Estate Agents

Relationships with other agents are also an important part of building your network. Even though you and the other agent might be on "opposite sides" of a transaction, you're still on the same team. You'll want to work together to make sure that the deal closes while keeping both of your clients happy.

You want to be known in the industry as someone who is easy to work with, friendly, and professional. On one particular deal, I was the buyer's agent and went above and beyond to keep the seller's agent informed throughout the entire process.

After the deal closed, the listing agent called me to let me know he had a three-family home going on the market and *allowed me to bring my buyers to view it prior to going on the market* and we had our offer accepted without any competition. Because of the great rapport from our first transaction, it led to special treatment on the next and a business relationship that continues to grow.

Last year, I was representing a buyer who didn't have the highest offer, but since I had a good relationship with the seller's agent, I was able to find out what their client's priorities were and win the deal. The sellers really needed a flexible closing date, so we offered to extend the closing for a month, which ended up being more important to the sellers than maximizing the sale price.

Another time, through a conversation with the listing agent, I found out that the sellers were elders and wanted to leave as much as they could in the house for the sale since they were unable to clear everything themselves. My buyers were willing to clear any personal items left behind and this made the deal much easier for the sellers to accept.

None of these deals would have been possible without building relationships and working with the agents on the other end of the deal. I always try to create a win-win situation when possible and make all parties happy with the transaction.

Chapter 10
Motivation & Confidence Building

In the real estate industry, confidence sells and the market is made up of sharks. If you lack confidence, you will be eaten alive!

Your clients will likely be interviewing two to three agents to represent them, so you *need* to learn how to stand out. People naturally gravitate toward people who are confident. This plays out in real estate too—the more confident you appear to clients, the more people will want to work with you and the more deals you will close.

You may not feel very confident yet as a new agent—but remember, confidence can be built by doing. The difference between the 75 percent of agents who quit in the first year and the 25 percent who push on? Persistence. And those who persist, get better and naturally gain more confidence.

When it comes to building confidence as an agent, I like to focus on these in particular: reputation, saying yes, celebrating wins, and investing in yourself.

You don't have control over the market, or how long it takes to sell your first home, but you do have control over how you present yourself and what you spend your time on.

Reputation

Reputation is *every*thing! How clients see you, how other agents see you, and how your community sees you all matter and will set you apart from other agents. Real estate is all about relationships. We are in the business of people.

Think about who *you* are and what your principles are and *write them down*. What do you stand for and you are willing to build your reputation on? What values do you want to be known for?

- Do you want to be known as a quick communicator? Do you want your clients to say, "Wow, if she answered my instagram DM that fast, imagine what it will be like for her to sell our home!"

- Do you want to create a reputation of being family-first, since you're a parent as well? Do you want your clients to know that it's okay to have their kids with them when touring homes, and that you know everything about the schools in the area?

- Do you want a reputation of being a community-first agent? Do you want your clients to know who you are because they've seen your face in smiling photos in local businesses, on postcards, or from a volunteer event?

Get crystal clear on what matters to you and make sure your actions follow. Your reputation might take a while to build, but it's quick to ruin if you start acting in ways that don't align with your values.

What do you want to be known for?

Jot down what you want to be known for. What are the first things that come to mind?

_____
_____
_____

Say Yes to Everything (in the beginning)

When you're just starting out, say yes to every opportunity presented to you. Everything you do is a stepping stone toward your future in real estate. Throw yourself into the fire, be brave (even when it's awkward or uncomfortable) and put yourself out there.

There are lots of opportunities to go to local events, young professionals meetups, coffee chats, or online networking calls. It's also important to attend events outside of the real industry to build up that network! If you need to practice speaking to people you don't know, these are great places to start.

You don't have to attend networking events forever, but they can help get you your first clients and network partners. When you go, don't forget to take pictures, post them on your social media accounts, and tag everyone you spoke to.

Research & write down two networking events you could go to in your area this month

_____
_____
_____

Celebrate Every Win

We can get so focused on our future goals that we skip over tracking and celebrating our progress and small wins along the way. If you are struggling with confidence, it can really make a huge difference if you begin to track and take notice of all your wins.

This practice can completely shift your mindset from, "I am so far from my goals" to "Wow, I've accomplished a lot more than I realized!"

Wins to celebrate:

- Getting your real estate license
- Signing with a brokerage
- First potential client reaching out
- First open house
- First home tour
- First offer accepted
- First home listed
- First offer negotiated
- First commission check

- Attending an event
- Presenting or training another agent
- Hitting daily goals
- Hitting quarterly goals
- Hitting your yearly goal
- Making progress toward any of your goals

Tracking *all* of your wins, both big and small, fuels motivation and empowers you to level up. If you make a habit of tracking these accomplishments, you will start to build more confidence!

Invest in Yourself

One of the best investments you can make? Is in yourself. We never stop learning, and reading this book is a perfect way for you to start this habit!

I truly believe that constant learning is the key to unlocking your full potential and building up your confidence. You can take extra classes to strengthen your skills, such as real estate or social media workshops. The more you learn, the better agent you'll become.

If you're looking to surround yourself with others on a similar path, go to **www.sheclosesdeals.com/community** to join my community of agents who are taking their businesses to the next level.

Dress the Part

In real estate, appearance matters. What you wear and how you look can make a big difference in whether or not potential clients choose to work with you.

Now don't get me wrong, you don't have to spend thousands of dollars on designer clothes to look the part. You just need to look professional and put together.

Dressing the part will also help with your confidence. Research shows that people who dress professionally and above the bare minimum not only have higher self-esteem, but also perform better at their jobs.[1]

Need ideas on what to wear? You can shop my go-to outfits for showings, open houses, & more at www.sheclosesdeals.com/closet

Get Professional Photos

As soon as I got licensed as a brand new agent, I had professional photos taken and not only did it improve my professional look online, but it made me feel more confident in myself.

If you're on a small budget, you can just pay for a couple of good headshots. But, if you are able to invest in 15–20 branding photos, you'll have plenty of high-quality, professional photos to use in your emails and social media posts.

My first photos were taken by a friend who had started a photography business and she gave me a "friend discount." Looking back, they weren't perfect, but I was able to use them to start marketing myself and standing out from my competition.

Branding shoots can cost between $250–$1,000 per session depending on the experience of the photographer and number of total photos. This kind of investment is highly valuable and worth it for you to become a multi-million dollar agent.

I take new branding photos multiple times per year so that I always have new content to post. If this sounds overwhelming, just start with getting your first session done. The first step is always the most difficult!

When I look back through all my old photos, I can see through my pictures how nervous I was in the early days and how I became more powerful and more confident in my more recent pictures as a top agent.

Believe In Your Own Success

If you read all the way to this point in the book, I know without a doubt that you truly want to become a successful, powerful real estate agent and that you already have the skills and the drive to make it happen. Your success is inevitable.

No one is going to believe in you more than yourself. I can give you every tool and bit of experience I have as an agent, but I can't motivate you to do the work. I can't believe it for you. You need to want it bad enough for yourself.

If you don't believe that you're capable of hitting your goals at this stage—as a new or newish agent—you won't believe it at any stage. You have to practice manifesting and believing that you are worthy and capable of becoming your own success story.

Manifestation isn't just about beliefs though. Manifestation is getting clear on your vision, your desires, staying positive, and matching those beliefs with your actions and hard work. Manifestation is simply putting your actions behind your words because you know what you're capable of.

Success doesn't just happen. Every day, I use a to-do list to match my actions with my goals. I typically make this list right before bed so that I can hit the ground running.

The next morning, I start with the most pressing tasks and work my way through my to-do list until everything is done. Throughout the day, I practice positive self-talk reminding myself that I am strong, powerful, and capable of greatness.

Completing this list has become part of my identity. I *always* do what I say I'm going to do and it's this work ethic that has set me apart and made me a top 1 percent agent.

Closing

With everything we've covered in this book, you may feel you have a lot to consider. Maybe you read parts of this book and wonder if you are cut out for the job of selling, negotiating, and keeping every part of the deal on track. Or, maybe you have a true passion for real estate but the idea of selling on social media and marketing to clients online feels impossible because your life isn't "aesthetic," or you don't have the connections to sell luxury properties (yet). If you look for reasons why you're not ready or you can't do it, you will find them. Everyone has obstacles; you have a choice in whether or not you let your obstacles define you.

As you finish out this book, I want to be a little vulnerable with you. If real estate exams were any indication of my real estate career, I should have failed on my very first day as an agent. But I did not fail because in the world of real estate, persistence wins over perfection every single time.

I have made so many embarrassing mistakes throughout my real estate career. I have lost out on deals. I've told clients things, only to learn later that I was completely wrong. I've had clients fire me. I've made dozens of cringe social media posts. The path to my real estate success has not been graceful or perfect. But, as Barbara Corcoran says, "Forget about perfection; it doesn't exist."[1]

I want to encourage you to do your absolute best and overdeliver for your clients. Go above and beyond. Treat everyone from your clients to your team like gold, and be a great human. Be honest and ethical, and fix your mistakes when you make them (because you will). What I have learned about being a real estate agent is that your success doesn't come from being "perfect"—it comes from how you build relationships with other people. People won't remember every detail from your 'Why Me' pitch or what you said during showings, but they will remember how you made them feel.

I also want you to know that where you live does not define your success or how much money you can make as a real estate agent. You don't need to live in a high-income city or sell million-dollar homes to make meaningful income in the industry, despite how the real estate industry is portrayed on TV and on social media. Most of the homes I sell in central Massachusetts are three-bedroom, 2.5-bath single-family homes in the $450–$500k range. The average square footage is 2,000. While I do work with investors, most of my clients are just regular people moving, buying, and selling homes. I share this to say that you can build a seven-figure real estate career simply by selling homes to families, or you can do it selling luxury high-rise condos. There are so many different paths to success and countless opportunities.

Throughout this book, I have laid out for you everything you need to know to have a fulfilling and exciting career in real estate and make millions along the way. I have used every single tip and strategy I outlined in this book to become a top agent. But the information I have given you is not enough. Just having the knowledge is never enough. It's what you do with it, and what you believe about yourself that will help you succeed.

With that in mind, I truly want to encourage you that if you feel called to a successful career in real estate, and you can visualize yourself thriving as a top real estate agent, take the leap and go all in. Every struggle and every challenge in your life up to this point has been preparing you for this. It is okay to be nervous, to have to do things more than once and to do them scared. I took my real estate exam about ten times, after all!

Know that it will not be easy, but building the life you envision is worth it. Know that you have people to support you who truly want to see you succeed (and if you don't have these people yet, go out and find them!). Pushing yourself to grow personally and professionally is uncomfortable, but you will never become the woman you are meant to be unless she is forced to come out!

I wish you all of the success in the world, but more than that, I hope that you enjoy the journey along the way.

Glossary

Adjustable-Rate Mortgage (ARM): A loan with an interest rate that can fluctuate over time.

Appraisal: A professional assessment of a property's value.

Buyer's Agreement: A contract between a buyer and a real estate agent outlining the terms of representation for the buyer.

Buyer's Questionnaire: A form used by real estate agents to gather information about a buyer's needs and budget.

Closing: The final meeting where ownership of the property is transferred.

Closing Costs: Fees associated with buying or selling a property, paid at closing.

Closing Date: The specific date on which the sale of a property is finalized.

Commission: The fee earned by a real estate agent for facilitating a real estate transaction. This is typically a percentage of the purchase price.

Contingency: A condition that must be met before a sale is finalized (e.g., financing, inspection).

CRM (Customer Relationship Management): Software used by real estate agents to manage client interactions and transactions.

Days on Market (DOM): The number of days a property has been listed for sale.

Deposits: Money paid upfront by a buyer to secure their interest in a property. This can include earnest money and escrow deposits.

Equity: The difference between a property's market value and the amount owed on the mortgage.

Escrow: An account holding funds (often down payment) until closing.

Expired Listings: Properties where the listing agreement with a seller has expired.

Fiduciary Duty: A legal obligation to act in the best interests of a client.

Financing: The process of securing a loan to purchase real estate.

Final Walkthrough: A final inspection of the property by the buyer before closing to ensure it's in the agreed-upon condition.

Home Inspection: A thorough examination of a property's condition by a qualified professional.

Inspection Period: A time frame in a purchase agreement where the buyer can have the property inspected for any issues.

Lease: A legal agreement outlining the terms of renting a property.

Listing Agent: A real estate agent who represents the seller in marketing and selling a property.

Listing Agreement: A contract between a seller and a real estate agent outlining the terms of representation.

Listing Appointments: Meetings with potential sellers to discuss listing their property.

MLS (Multiple Listing Service): A database of properties for sale, shared by cooperating real estate agents.

MLS Quarterly Fees: Fees paid by real estate agents to participate in the MLS.

Mortgage: A loan secured by real estate, used to finance its purchase.

Mortgage Type and What % Down Payment: There are various mortgage types (e.g., fixed-rate, adjustable-rate) with different qualifying down payment percentages (e.g., FHA loans may require lower down payments).

NAR (National Association of Realtors): A trade association for real estate professionals in the United States.

Offer: A formal proposal from a buyer to purchase a property at a specific price and terms.

Offer Expiration: The date and time by which a buyer's offer becomes null and void if not accepted by the seller.

Open House: A public event where potential buyers can tour a property for sale.

P & S (Purchase and Sale Agreement): A legal document outlining the terms of a real estate transaction, signed by both buyer and seller.

P&S Date: The date on which the buyer and seller sign the Purchase and Sale Agreement.

Pre-Approval: A lender's conditional commitment to provide a mortgage up to a certain amount.

Property Disclosure: A document informing potential buyers of a property's known defects.

Real Estate Agent: A licensed professional who assists buyers and sellers with real estate transactions.

Real Estate Brokerage: A company that employs real estate agents and facilitates real estate transactions.

Real Estate Farming: Targeted marketing efforts directed at a specific geographic area to generate seller and buyer leads.

Real Estate License: A government-issued permit required to practice real estate as an agent or broker.

Realtor®: A real estate agent who is a member of the National Association of Realtors (NAR).

Realtor Dues: Membership fees paid by real estate agents to belong to the National Association of Realtors (NAR).

Title: Legal ownership of a property.

Title Search: An investigation to verify ownership and identify any claims on a property's title.

Notes

Introduction

1. National Association of Realtors. "NAR Reaches Agreement to Resolve Nationwide Claims Brought by Home Sellers." Last modified October 4, 2023._https://www.nar.realtor/newsroom/nar-reaches-agreement-to-resolve-nationwide-claims-brought-by-home-sellers.

2. LaPonsie, Maryalene. "How Lawsuits Could Impact Real Estate Commissions." Bankrate, March 28, 2023. https://www.bankrate.com/real-estate/real-estate-commissions-lawsuit-impact/#nar-lawsuit.

Chapter 2

1. Entrepreneur. "12 Quotes from Barbara Corcoran on Success, Failure, and More." Entrepreneur Magazine. Accessed March 15, 2024 https://www.entrepreneur.com/leadership/12-quotes-from-barbara-corcoran-on-success-failure/290006.

2. Tracy Tutor. "MDLLA's Tracy Tutor on Her Career Journey, Embracing Failures, and What's Next." Bravo TV, The Daily Dish. Accessed March 15, 2024._https://www.bravotv.com/the-daily-dish/mdlla-tracy-tutor-on-her-career-journey-exclusive-details.

3. Chris Miller. "Why Do So Many Realtors Fail? (And How Not To)." The Close, February 6, 2023._https://theclose.com/why-realtors-fail/.

Chapter 6

1. Maya Vander. "Selling Sunset's Maya Vander on Balancing Motherhood & Real Estate, Her Growing Family & Her Hopes for Season 5."

Interview by Brianne Hogan. SheKnows, December 1, 2021. https://www.sheknows.com/feature/selling-sunset-maya-vander-interview-2561926/.

2. Emma Hernan. "Emma Hernan on Her Selling Sunset Success and Her Best Career Advice." Interview by Jessica Bailey. Grazia, April 14, 2022. https://graziamagazine.com/me/articles/career-advice-emma-hernan-selling-sunset/.

Chapter 7

1. Samantha DeBianchi. "'Million Dollar Listing Miami' Star Samantha DeBianchi Talks Show's Premiere, Career Tips and Why the Magic City Is a Hot Real Estate Market." Interview by Tony Maglio. TheWrap, June 25, 2014._https://www.thewrap.com/bravo-million-dollar-listing-miami-samantha-debianchi-interview/.

Chapter 8

1. Jade Mills. "Coldwell Banker's Jade Mills: An Archetype for Success." Interview by Aly J. Yale. RealtyBizNews, March 10, 2016. https://realtybiznews.com/coldwell-bankers-jade-mills-an-archetype-for-success/98775874/.

2. "Zillow Sued Over 'Zestimate'." Chicago Real Estate Source, May 19, 2017. https://www.chicagorealestatesource.com/blog/zillow-sued-over-zestimate/.

3. Mandy Kennon. "Scents That Make Sense When Selling Your Home." U.S. News & World Report, January 26, 2018._https://realestate.usnews.com/real-estate/articles/scents-that-make-sense-when-selling-your-home.

4. National Association of Realtors. "Highlights from the Profile of Home Buyers and Sellers." Last modified 2023._https://www.nar.realtor/research-and-statistics/research-reports/highlights-from-the-profile-of-home-buyers-and-sellers.

Chapter 9

1. Jacob Klein. "When You Look Good, You Feel Good. Research Shows You Might Even Be More Productive." Temple University News, June 1, 2023.__https://news.temple.edu/news/2023-06-01/

when-you-look-good-you-feel-good-research-shows-you-might-even-be-more-productive.

Closing

1. Entrepreneur. "12 Quotes from Barbara Corcoran on Success, Failure, and More." Entrepreneur Magazine. Accessed March 15, 2024 https://www.entrepreneur.com/leadership/12-quotes-from-barbara-corcoran-on-success-failure/290006.

30-Day Challenge

Congratulations on taking the first steps towards a fulfilling career in real estate!

To help you make your dreams happen, I put together this 30-Day Challenge. You'll get daily action steps to build your knowledge, network, and confidence. Each day offers a bite-sized task you can complete in minutes, designed to move you forward and keep you motivated. You can do this before you get your real estate license, or even as a licensed agent.

All of the action steps are repeatable too - I do many of these things over and over again if I need a confidence boost or need to expand my network!

Why a 30-Day Challenge?

Small, consistent actions lead to big results. This challenge is all about building momentum and creating positive habits that will empower you to be successful in real estate.

How to Take the Challenge:

1. Visit **www.sheclosesdeals.com/challenge** to get the daily prompts. Each day, there is a new action-based prompt in the challenge.

2. Track your progress: Use a journal, planner, or this tracker to mark your daily accomplishments. Celebrate your progress and stay motivated!

3. Tag me @brookeecoughlin on Instagram in your posts to share your progress with our real estate agent community. Let's do it together!

Here's a sneak peek of what you can expect each week in the challenge!

Week 1: Building Your Foundation

- Set goals for the next year.
- Learn key real estate terms.
- Start a motivational book in real estate.
- Research top brokerages in your city.
- Attend an open house and observe the agent's strategies.

Week 2: Networking & Visibility

- Have Coffee with an Agent or Broker.
- Write your "Why Me" pitch to practice selling yourself as an agent.
- Practice and refine your pitch for confident delivery.
- Share your most recent win on social media.
- Write a positive review for a local business you love.

Week 3: Sharpening Your Skills

- Take a free online class to expand your real estate knowledge.
- Become a local expert by learning about a specific neighborhood.
- Shadow a successful agent to gain invaluable insights.
- Take a virtual tour of a luxury property and practice what you would say if you were the agent showing the home.
- Practice negotiation skills in a non-real estate area of your life.

Week 4: Building Your Personal Brand

- Plan your weekly to-do list.
- Support a small business & tag them on your social media.
- Ask a local agent if you can assist at their open house.
- Write a letter to your future self. Reflect on your goals and aspirations; visualize your successful real estate career.
- Put on a nice outfit & do your hair today.

Plus Bonus Self-Care Activities Sprinkled Throughout the Challenge, including:

- Listen to an uplifting playlist.

- Meditate or write down 5 things you're grateful for.

- Work out today.

- Drink water & take a long walk.

- Try an exercise class you've never done before.

Remember: Track your progress and celebrate your wins! Visit **www.shecloses-deals.com/challenge** for more details and resources.

Real Estate Scripts

In the following pages of this book, you will find 50+ of my exact scripts of what I say to clients, network partners, and other agents in all of my day-to-day real estate situations. You can customize these to fit your personal brand and use them again and again.

You can also download the entire list of real estate scripts as a note you can save to your phone (which is how I use them) so that all you need to do is just copy & paste any time you are texting or emailing your clients!

Visit **www.sheclosesdeals.com/scripts** to get all my exact scripts as a note on your phone!

Social Media Scripts

You can use these scripts for your social media posts!

How to Introduce Yourself on Social Media

It's a good idea, especially if you are a new agent, to record a short video introducing yourself and pin it to the top of your social media profiles. Here's what I say, feel free to customize it to fit your style! (I have included a customizable template below my example).

Hello everybody. I'm Brooke Coughlin, from Byrnes Real Estate Group. Here's a little bit about myself. I'm a top agent in Massachusetts, Connecticut and Rhode Island closing over $30 million worth of real estate this past year, over 50 transactions. In addition to helping people buy and sell, I also am a personal investor owning a multi-million dollar real estate portfolio. In that portfolio, I also have Airbnbs, and I also co-own an Airbnb management company.

To go along with that, I also own a six-figure cleaning company as well with the best team in the world. Before this, I was a 7th grade English teacher. I like to say I used to teach seventh graders but now I teach adults on how to buy & sell. So, let's connect!

Here's the script:

Hello everybody. I'm [your name] from [your brokerage]. Here's a little bit about me.
I'm an agent in [state or area],

[closing over $30 million worth of real estate this past year, over 50 transactions]

(share either 1) your numbers, or 2) your niche. Ex. "specializing in new builds" or "working with first time home buyers.")

In addition to helping people buy and sell, I also [personal or business accomplishments].

(Share something that makes people want to connect with you. It could be another business you own, your former career, your hobbies, that you are a mom, etc.)

I would love to help you buy or sell in [area], let's connect.

Video Home Tour Script

I used this exact script for all of my homes, from small, starter homes or fixer uppers to luxury million-dollar properties!

Hello everybody, this is [Your Name] from [Your Brokerage]. Welcome to my newest listing at [123 Main Street]. X beds, X baths, X amount of square footage.

[Unique selling points of the home]

Let's check it out!"

I like to point out a few unique features of the home. For example, at one of my recent new listings, the seller lived in the home for 58 years so I added, "this home has been meticulously kept by the same owner for the past 58 years!"

Social Media 'Why ME" Pitch - New Agent

This is very similar to the "why me" pitch you would give in person at a listing appointment, just slightly shorter for posting to your social media!

Looking to buy or sell?

Value of working with me, [Your Name]:

- 24/7 open communication
- Marketing exposure on 500+ websites
- Showtime 24 hour appointment center, lock boxes, & open houses
- Breakdown of the buying & selling process
- Inspector, lawyer, & lender connections
- Staging connections
- FREE professional photography
- FREE moving truck
- FREE professional deep cleaning

Call or text me today to get started on your adventure! [phone number]

[Your Name]

[Realtor or Real Estate Agent]

[Your Brokerage]

C: [phone]

F: [fax]

[Website]

[Email]

[Physical Mailing Address]

Social Media 'Why ME" Pitch - Established Agent

Looking to buy or sell?

Value of Buying or Selling With [Your Name]:

- Top Realtor in X Counties
- Multi-million dollar producing broker
- 24/7 open communication via call, text, email, in-person meetings
- Extensive market knowledge
- Expert negotiator
- Breakdown of the buying and selling process
- Top marketing exposure and your property will be sent out via email to our network of over 5,000 potential buyers
- Neighborhood Flyers in 2-Mile Radius
- Hard Money Connections
- Lock boxes & open houses
- FREE professional photography and videography
- FREE deep house cleaning prior to listing
- Lender, Lawyer, Inspector, Contractor, & Staging Connections

My goal is to make your transaction as seamless as possible and make you the most money possible!

[Your Name]

[Realtor or Real Estate Agent]

[Your Brokerage]

C: [phone]

F: [fax]

[Website]

[Email]

[Physical Mailing Address]

Networking and Professional Connection Scripts

These simple scripts can help you make connections and find people to be on your team!

How to Introduce Yourself at Networking Events

When you introduce yourself in person, you want to keep what you say "short and sweet" but also come across as confident. That's why I always use my first and last name, my brokerage name, and tell them something about me. As a more established agent, I use my numbers, but if you are new, the best thing is to share who you help.

Hi, I'm [your full name] from [your real estate broker].

I'm an agent in [state or area], [closing over $30 million worth of real estate this past year, over 50 transactions]

(share either 1) your numbers, or 2) your niche. Ex. "specializing in new builds" or "working with first time home buyers.")

Network Connection Request - Text or Email

Here's my script for making a network connection with a professional in your industry:

Hello [Name],

I hope this message finds you well! I've been following your work in the [industry/field] and I'm genuinely impressed by your expertise and achievements. As a [new, recent, established] real estate agent, I'm passionate about staying current and building strong, collaborative relationships within our industry.

I'm reaching out to see if you'd be open to a brief virtual meeting or phone call in the coming weeks. I'm eager to learn more about your insights and experiences, and to explore how we might support each other's goals and initiatives.
If you're interested, please let me know a few days and times that work for you, and we can arrange a convenient time to connect. I'm looking forward to the opportunity to chat with you!

Best regards,
[Your Name]

Coffee Chat Request - Text or Email

Hello [Name].

I have been following you and your business for quite some time now and I am very impressed. I am a newer agent in the real estate industry and I am looking to grow my team. Would you have time to grab coffee in the next few weeks? I would love to learn more about your business, offerings and how we could potentially build a working relationship together.

Let me know a few days and times that work on your end. I look forward to chatting with you!

Best, [Your Name]

Buyer Interaction Scripts

These are the exact scripts I use every day when working with home buyers and potential new clients!

Welcome Text to Home Buyers

Hi [client first name]! How have we connected?

I always like to know where the lead or connection comes from. This helps you learn which of your social media channels or your referrals are sending you leads so you can continue to focus on those.

Next, your goal should be to build up the client's excitement of getting ready to purchase a home. Here's what I say:

Super exciting that you are getting ready to purchase a new home. You are in great hands with me, and I will take care of you each step of the way. I do have a few questions to help get you started on your search.

Prospective Buyer Client Questionnaire

Typically I do this questionnaire over the phone but you can also send this via text or email, depending on what your client prefers.

1. What is your current living situation? (Renting/in a lease, homeowner and need to sell, living with parents, etc.)

2. Have you been pre-approved? If yes, what is your maximum budget where you feel comfortable at?

3. What towns are you interested in?

4. Any specifics such as numbers of beds/baths/sq footage, privacy, needing a neighborhood/garage, etc.?

5. Anything you hate and want to stay away from?

6. Are you looking for something turnkey or are you willing to put sweat equity in?

7. What is your ideal timeline? Are you ready tomorrow if the perfect house pops up on the market or are you in no rush?

8. Can I have your email address and best contact information to set you up on an email search?

You will start receiving daily emails from me with homes that match your criteria. If and when any pop up that spur your interest, just give me a call and we can schedule a time to go and see it.

I look forward to working with you on this journey!

Sending a Listing to a Potential Client or Client

Even once I have set my buyer client up with an automated MLS search, I still check the MLS every single day for any properties that might match their search and if I find something, I personally send it to them in an email. This shows them I really care and I'm going the extra mile for my clients. You can even do this with potential clients who haven't fully committed to a home search yet as a way to get their attention. Here's what you can put in your email:

Hi [Client name],

I know that you're looking for a property with [name their top 1-2 priorities], so this home might check off all your boxes!

[link to the listing]
Take a look, let me know what you think, and if you'd like to set up a showing!

Have a great day!
[Your Name]

Showings - Text/Email to Seller's Agent

Hello [agent name], this is [your name] from [Brokerage]. Can I please show your listing at [123 Main Street] on [date] and time]?

Running Buyer's Potential Numbers with Lenders - Text

I like to put my clients in a group text with the lender and myself so we are all on the same page. I can ask my lenders to run hypothetical numbers for my clients immediately while we are touring a home, so they have a clear idea of what they'd be paying.

Hey _____ [lender name], [Buyer Name] is interested in [123 Main Street]. We would be offering 500k with 20% down and the taxes are $5,000 a year. What would his/her monthly payment look like?

What to say to wrap up a showing - In Person

If the showing has gone well and I can sense my clients are excited and interested, here's exactly what I say to avoid putting pressure on them right away to make an offer.

Hey guys, I can tell you really love it here. Take the drive home and talk about it. We can also text your lender and have them run the numbers so you know what your monthly payment would look like.

Remember, we always want you to be comfortable. If you think of any additional questions, send them my way. I could really see you guys here in this house!

Putting in an Offer - Text to Seller's Agent

If I am representing a buyer and my client wants to put in an offer on the home, I let the seller's agent know right away that my buyer is interested and an offer is coming, so they do not accept any competing contracts before they receive my client's offer!

I send this quick text to the seller's agent,

"Hi [seller's agent]. I just showed your listing at 123 Main Street. My buyers are definitely in love. Can you let me know if there is anything specific your sellers are looking for and if you have any offers on the table? I am on the road for the afternoon but an offer will be coming by later tonight. Thanks!".

Putting in an Offer - Email to Seller's Agent

Hello [agent's name],

Thank you for allowing me to show [123 Main Street] today. It checks all of the boxes for my client. Please see our strong offer attached.

Documents Included:
(List documents that are attached in the offer package)

- Offer to purchase
- Pre-approval
- Lead paint disclosure
- Seller disclosures

Highlights of Offer:

- $500,000 purchase price
- $20,000 deposit
- Offer valid until tomorrow at noon (always be aggressive)
- 2/15 purchase and sale date
- 3/1 closing date
- 25% down conventional financing with my preferred lender

- Inspections for informational purposes only
- All appliances to stay

My client, lender, attorney, and myself are very easy to work with. Please confirm receipt and let me know if you have any questions. I would love to co-broke with you on this transaction.

Best,
[Your name]

What to say to Buyers with Cold Feet - Text, In Person, or Phone Call

More often than not, you will talk first time homebuyers off a ledge. When they wonder, "Did I make the right decision?" I try to first point out all of the good attributes of the home. This includes newer, bigger ticket items like roof, heating systems, location, and how many boxes of the home checked off from their list.

Then I say,

Getting cold feet is normal as buying a home is a massive investment. But with no risk, there is no reward and this is as good of a risk you will find!

What to say to Buyers at a Bad Inspection - Text, In Person, or Phone Call

I am very honest with my clients. If the inspection was horrible, I do not hide my thoughts on that as I would never want my clients to get into a bad investment (although sometimes I have shared my thoughts and they purchased the home anyway).

Here's what I say:

Hi [Client's Name], I hope you're doing well. I wanted to talk to you about the inspection report we received for the property at [Property Address]. To be completely transparent, the findings were not as favorable as we had hoped.

There were several significant issues identified, including [mention a few key problems, e.g., structural damage, outdated electrical systems, mold]. These are not just cosmetic issues; they could potentially lead to costly repairs and might even impact the safety and value of the home.

I understand that this property might have some appealing features, but the inspection suggests that this could be a bad investment.

Ultimately, it's your decision. If you're still interested in the property, we can certainly move forward. However, I would recommend negotiating with the seller to address these issues or to lower the price to account for the needed repairs. My priority is to ensure that you have all the info you need to make the best decision for you and your family, and that you're happy with your investment in the long run.

What to say to Seller's Agent if Buyers Back Out -Text

If your Buyer Clients want to negotiate a reduced price:

Hello [agent name]. After the inspections there were quite a few bigger ticket items that popped up that my buyer is uneasy with. We are requesting a credit of X [dollar amount] at closing to take care of the following items post closing or to have the seller take care of them with a licensed professional with proof of invoices. My buyer really does want to make this work, however these items are non-negotiables.

I have found credit at closings are typically better than reduced purchase price for less money out of pocket for your clients at the closing table. A $10,000 credit goes a lot further than dropping the price by $10,000 over a 30-year loan. If your Buyer Clients are not comfortable with the inspection & want to back out:

Hello [agent name].

Unfortunately after inspections my buyer no longer will be moving forward with the transaction. Just so you are aware the bigger ticket items that popped up were X, X and X [list major issues]. I am sending along the release now. I wish you the best of luck and hope our paths cross again soon!

What to say to Buyers at a Good Inspection - Text, In Person, or Phone Call

This was one of the cleanest inspections I have been to. Based on the inspection and market trends, this property seems like a solid investment with good potential for future appreciation. There are no guarantees, but based on the market, you could feel confident about this asset.

When a Buyer says, "What if a better home comes on the market?"

That's a very valid question! Just like in life and settling down with a partner, you could go with something that really makes you happy or you could miss out on something wonderful because you were waiting for the perfect situation.

Weekly Text to Buyers - Under Contract

This is the set of updates I send to my clients once we have an offer accepted and we are under contract. Most closings are on a 45-Day Timeline, so these texts are typically sent out over 4-6 weeks, but you can adjust to fit any timeline. You can send this via text or email. I typically text my clients every Monday with a weekly update, but you can do this on any day of the week.

Under Contract - Text

*Send this text when your clients' offer has been **Accepted**.*

Happy [day of the week]! Congratulations on your accepted offer. Here are the next steps:

- Who would you like to use as an attorney? I recommend [X person from X attorney's office]. I will send the fully signed offer over to your attorney of choice and your lender and will CC you on the email.

- Your first deposit is due. I will send over a deposit link for this. The seller's agent will hold it in their brokerage's escrow account.

- We have [X number] days for the inspection period. Remember, you can walk away for any reason during this time period without repercussions. Once we make it past inspections, you cannot back out. Do you have a home inspector you would like to use? If not, I have a list of them that I highly recommend. Please let me know a few days and times that work for you and I will cross check with my schedule and the inspector's schedule. The inspector will send you a breakdown of inspections you can have done and costs per each.

- Purchase and sale signing date is [X date]. A purchase and sale is a longer form of the offer itself. Your attorney and seller's attorney will draft this and your attorney will review it with you prior to signing. After this is signed, your second deposit of [X amount] is due and we are moving smoothly along!

These are the next steps we need to focus on. If you have any questions in the meantime do not hesitate to reach out.

Week 1 Update - Text

Happy Monday! Updates in your transaction:

- First deposit has been sent in
- Inspection period has passed and we are moving forward
- P&S has been signed
- Second deposit has been sent in
- We have ordered the appraisal and the appraiser will schedule this with the seller's agent.

- You will be working with your lender on mortgage commitment. Anything your lender requests, please get back to them in a timely manner. We have until [X date] for this.

These are the next steps we need to focus on. If you have any questions in the meantime do not hesitate to reach out.

Week 2 Update - Text

Happy Monday! Updates in your transaction:

- Appraisal has been taken care of. Just waiting on the green light from your lender on what the property appraised at.

- Again, continue working with your lender on mortgage commitment which is due on [X date].

These are the next steps we need to focus on. If you have any questions in the meantime, do not hesitate to reach out.

Week 3 Update - Text

Happy Monday, [Client name]! Updates in your transaction:

- Property appraised

- We have mortgage commitment

- Prepare for the final walk through. What day and time work on your end for this?

We will be making sure the house is in the same shape it was the last time you saw it. That all appliances are left behind, no leaks, no flooded basement etc. The Seller will leave any additional keys, garage door openers, any helpful information behind on the counter for you.

You will also want to schedule to have your utilities turned on for closing day. This includes your electricity, the provider is [electric company], heating and your provider is [gas heating company], internet/wifi and provider is [internet company], trash and the provider is [trash service company].

You will also want to go to the post office and change your address to your new home. I always also recommend buying new locks to change out. You never know who has copies of the current keys, and safety is always first!

I will also be your personal photographer to take a great memory photo with a sold sign in front of the house.

The day before closing, you will most likely get the final amount for the check you need to bring to closing. You will need to get a bank-certified check made out to the attorneys office. Always bring a personal check with you to closing in case the numbers fluctuate. And do not forget your ID!

Closing day!!! Closing is scheduled for [X day] at [X time]. You will need to bring the bank-certified check, a personal check, and your license. Your attorney will walk you through a stack of papers and you will need to sign your name 100 times LOL. If you have any questions now would be the time to ask, as after you sign you will own the home. The attorney then submits the house on record which takes about an hour from signing and then you are officially a new home owner.

These are the next steps we need to focus on. If you have any questions in the meantime do not hesitate to reach out. We are almost there!

Week 4 Update - Text

HAPPY CLOSING WEEK! Reminder: the final walk through is [X date] at [X time] and closing is scheduled for [X date] at [X time]. We are at the finish line. If you have any questions, just let me know!

Seller Interaction Scripts

These are scripts for the most common conversations and interactions you will have with sellers!

Welcome Text to Home Sellers

Hi [client first name]! How have we connected?

As I said for buyer clients, it's always good to know where the lead or connection comes from. This helps you learn which of your social media channels or your referrals are sending you leads so you can continue to focus on those.

Then, I typically say,

Super exciting that you are getting ready to sell your home. Now is a great time to sell! You are in great hands with me, and I will take care of you each step of the way. Our first step together is to schedule a time when I can come to your home and meet you and get a tour, and we can talk numbers! What is a good day and time for you?

Seller Questionnaire Script

I do this in person after doing a walkthrough of the client's home.

1. Why are you looking to sell and where are you hoping to go?
2. Style of home?
3. Year built?
4. Bought in what year and for what amount?*
5. Lot size? Property line?
6. Total square footage?
7. Number of bedrooms?
8. Number of bathrooms?

9. Laundry situation?

10. Heat type? Central air?

11. Age of heating systems?

12. Age of hot water heaters?

13. Foundation type?

14. Garage?

15. Number of parking spaces in the driveway?

16. What appliances will stay?

17. Public water and public sewer?

18. If private - Title V done? Date septic last pumped?

19. Age of roof or when was it last done?

20. Any seepage in the basement? Sump pump?

21. Age of windows?

22. Updates since purchased?

23. Any exclusions on the sale?

24. Any disclosures? Anything wrong with the home I should be aware of? Radon? Mold? Insects?

25. HOA fees?

26. Generator?

27. Solar panels?

28. Video/audio recording in your home?

29. Specific date you want to close on or before?

30. Showings/open houses availability?

31. Favorite part of the town? (It's important to know details of the town itself like schools, restaurants, crime rate etc)

32. Favorite part about the house?

Why Me Pitch

I tell my Clients, "There are a million realtors in the business and why should YOU work with ME?"

In order for clients to trust you enough to sell their home for them, you have to come across with confidence and know why someone should hire you. As a new agent, you need to practice this speech again and again before you ever have a seller client.

Write it out as a script and practice saying it out loud. Then, practice saying it in front of a mirror if you are struggling with confidence. You can also practice with other people. Ask a fellow new agent or a friend to let you practice selling yourself to them.

Even if you are a new agent, you have selling points! Here's a script you can use, even if you are brand new. Make a list of all of the selling points and connections you have to offer and customize the script below.

New Agent 'Why Me' Script

Value of Buying or Selling With [Your Name]:

- 24/7 open communication
- Marketing exposure on 500+ websites
- Showtime 24-hour appointment center, lock
- boxes & open houses
- Breakdown of the buying & selling process
- Inspector, lawyer & lender connections
- Staging connections
- FREE professional photography
- FREE moving truck
- FREE professional deep cleaning

[Your Name]

[Realtor or Real Estate Agent]

[Your Brokerage]

C: [phone]

F: [fax]

[Website]

[Email]

[Physical Mailing Address]

My goal is to make your transaction as seamless as possible and make you the most money possible!

The script above is the EXACT one I used as a new agent. Once I started selling more, I changed my speech to show more credibility. The one I use now is below.

Established Agent 'Why Me' Script

Value of Buying or Selling With [Your Name]:

- Top 1% Realtor in X Counties
- Multi-million dollar producing broker
- 24/7 open communication via call, text, email, in person meetings
- Extensive market knowledge
- Expert negotiator
- Breakdown of the buying and selling process
- Top marketing exposure and your property will be sent out via email to our network of over 5,000 potential buyers
- Neighborhood Flyers in 2-Mile Radius
- Hard Money Connections
- Lock boxes & open houses
- FREE professional photography and videography

- FREE deep house cleaning prior to listing
- Lender, Lawyer, Inspector, Contractor & Staging Connections

My goal is to make your transaction as seamless as possible and make you the most money possible!

[Your Name]

[Realtor or Real Estate Agent]

[Your Brokerage]

C: [phone]

F: [fax]

[Website]

[Email]

[Physical Mailing Address]

Follow up after Listing Appointments - Text

Hello ___ [Client name]. It was so wonderful meeting you and seeing your home. I would love nothing more than to work with you and for you on closing out this chapter and starting your new one! Please let me know if you have any additional questions and I am ready to roll when you are.

What to Say when Negotiating Deals for Sellers - Text to Buyer's Agent

After an open house, if there are multiple offers on the table, I typically call all of the buyers' agents and ask for the highest and best offers. I say to buyers' agents,

We are reviewing all offers. If your client would like to submit a new highest and best offer please let me know by X [date and time.]

Or I will say,

Look, my client really likes your offer and there is another offer that is very similar. If you can come up to X [amount], the property is yours.

What to Say to Buyers Whose Offers Were NOT Accepted - Text

Here is what I say to the buyer's agents whose offers were not accepted,

Thank you very much for your offer and if anything happens, I will gladly let you know. I hope our paths cross again in the future.

If there were multiple offers on the table, I sometimes like to add to the message,

There were X amount of offers on the table."

This helps the buyer's agent relay information to their clients. Remember, a good reputation is important and you want buyer's agents to want to work with you!

How to Suggest Reducing Sale Price - In Person or Phone Call

I've been reviewing the market trends and recent sales in our area, and I wanted to discuss the pricing strategy for your property.

Based on the current market conditions and the feedback we've received from potential buyers, I believe it might be beneficial to consider adjusting the sale price of your home.

While your property has many great features, a slight reduction in the price could make it more competitive and attract more interest.
I think we should reduce the price by [specific percentage or dollar $ amount]. This adjustment would position your property more favorably compared to similar homes in the area and could help expedite the sale process. Ultimately,

this is your decision, so take your time, but I'm here to support you! If you have any questions or need more information, please let me know.

When Sellers Worry They Accepted an Offer too Soon

I completely understand where you're coming from. It's natural to think about the "what ifs" with such an important decision. While there's always a chance that you could have gotten a higher offer, there's also a risk of the market shifting and potentially receiving lower offers in the future. We accepted an offer that was competitive and aligned with your goals and the property's value.

Weekly Text to Sellers - Under Contract

This is the set of updates I send to my clients once we have accepted an offer on their home and we are under contract. Most closings are on a 45-Day Timeline, so these texts are typically sent out over 4-6 weeks, but you can adjust to fit any timeline. You can send this via text or email. I typically text my clients every Monday with a weekly update, but you can do this on any day of the week.

Under Contract - Text

*Right after an **accepted** offer on the selling side I text my clients,*

Happy [day of the week]! Congratulations on accepting a fantastic offer on your home. Here are the next steps:

- Who would you like to use as an attorney? I recommend [X person from X attorney's office]. I will send the fully signed offer over to your attorney of choice and will cc you on the email.

The buyer's first deposit is due. I will send the buyer's agent a link for their deposit. I hold it in my brokerage's escrow account.

- The buyers have [X number] days for their inspection period. Remember, they can walk away for any reason during this time period without repercussions. Once we make it past inspections, we are over the biggest hurdle. I will let you know what day and time the inspection is scheduled for. You should not be home for this. Please do your best to make your house as tidy as it was when we were on the market!

- Purchase and sale signing date is [X date]. A purchase and sale is a longer form of the offer itself. Your attorney and the buyers' attorney will draft this and your attorney will review it with you prior to signing.

- After this is signed, the buyer's second deposit of [X amount] is due.

- We are moving smoothly along!

These are the next steps we need to focus on. If you have any questions in the meantime do not hesitate to reach out.

Week 1 Update - Text

Happy Monday! Updates in your transaction:

- First deposit in hand

- Inspection period has passed

- P&S has been signed

- Second deposit in hand

- I should be hearing any day now from the appraiser. I will let you know when this is scheduled for. I will meet the appraiser at your home and will come ready to roll with comps and everything needed to push this transaction along.

- Buyers are still working on mortgage commitment. They have until [X date] for this.

These are the next steps we need to focus on. If you have any questions in the meantime, please do not hesitate to reach out.

Week 2 Update - Text

Happy Monday. Updates in your transaction:

- Appraisal has been taken care of. Just waiting on the green light from the buyer's agent that the property appraised.

- Again, just waiting on the buyer's mortgage commitment which is due on [X date].

- We will need a smoke certificate prior to closing. Please call the town fire department and request a smoke alarm inspection. This is typically $50 per town (can vary based on type of home and location). If you have any concerns with your smoke alarms / carbon monoxide detectors please let me know and I can connect you with [recommended expert] who can come take a peek and make any updates needed prior to the fire department coming out. I recommend doing this sooner rather than later in case there are any hiccups.

These are the next steps we need to focus on. If you have any questions in the meantime, please do not hesitate to reach out.

Week 3 Update - Text

Happy Monday. Updates in your transaction:

- Property appraised

- Buyers have mortgage commitment

- Smoke certificate has been completed

- Prepare for the final walk through. Buyers are planning on doing their final walk through on [X date] at [X time]. The house will need to be empty for this and in broom swept condition. Please leave any additional keys, garage door openers, any helpful information behind on the counter for the new owner. You will also want to schedule to have your utilities turned off for closing day

- Closing day!! Buyers are signing at [X day] at [X time]. Your home should be officially sold by [X time].

These are the next steps we need to focus on. If you have any questions in the meantime, please do not hesitate to reach out. We are almost there!

Week 4 Update - Text

HAPPY CLOSING WEEK! This is your reminder that the final walk through is on [X date] at [X time] and closing is scheduled for [X date] at [X time]. We are at the finish line. If you have any questions just let me know!

Open House Scripts

These scripts will help you with everything you need to say during & after an open house!

What to Say to Potential Buyers at an Open House

I greet all potential buyers with this intro:

Happy Sunday! Welcome to 123 Main Street. I am Brooke from Byrnes Real Estate Group. If you don't mind signing in for me, that would be great. I will gladly give you some information on the property, and then you have free rein to walk around, and I'm here for questions!

- Price point
- Beds/baths
- Square footage
- Acreage
- Recent updates
- Favorite features of the property

Go enjoy!! Here if you need me!

Then in a casual, friendly conversation, after they've toured the home, I ask these questions,

- How long have you been looking for a home?
- Are you working with an agent? If so, who?

- Does this house check all of your boxes and if it does not, what are you looking for? Maybe I can make a recommendation.

Follow Up Post-Open House for New Leads

Hello ____ this is [your name] from [your brokerage]. Thank you for coming to my open house at [123 Main Street] this weekend. Do you have any further questions I can answer or further interest to pursue? If this home wasn't the one for you I would be happy to help you find the one that is.

Past Client Engagement Scripts

Staying in touch with past clients is extremely important but it doesn't have to be awkward! These scripts will help you stay connected to past clients so they will keep recommending you again and again.

Review Request - Text

Hello [client name],

How is everything going? I hope you and your family are enjoying your new home

I am honored to have assisted you in your transaction and wish you nothing but the absolute best.

If and when you have a second, I would appreciate it if you could write me a quick review that I can share on social media with past, present and future clients.

If you click the link below, it will bring you to my Facebook page. Click on reviews, and you can write your own! (If you could make it public that would be ideal)

Review here: [link to your facebook or google profile]

I would appreciate any feedback!

Here are some things to think about:

1. How the transaction went from start to finish

2. My knowledge in the real estate field

3. My communication levels

4. If you would recommend our services to others

5. How many stars would you rate your experience

Feel free to use all or any of the above suggestions.

I appreciate you and your business and I will always just be a phone call away if you need me!

Referral Request - Text

I text this to my clients and everyone in my contacts list 4 times per year and customize the text for the season!

HAPPY [season]!

Wishing you and your family the best year yet filled with happiness, health, success and maybe a new home? For the first quarter of the year, I [your name and your brokerage] will be offering a [incentive, ex. $250 gift card to Home Goods or Home Depot] if you close on a property with me from now until the end of [end of the month/year]. You can also win a $250 gift card if you refer me to any friend or family member who closes in the first quarter.

As always, if you are looking to buy, sell, invest or build with top notch service, I am just a quick text away! Cheers!

Holiday Message to Past Clients - Text

You can customize this for every holiday! Remember you want to stay top of mind for your past, present, and future clients!

Hi [Client's Name]

Wishing you and your loved ones a joyful Christmas season filled with warmth, happiness, and cherished moments. As we celebrate this special time of year, I want to express my heartfelt gratitude for your trust and support. As always, if you are looking to buy, sell, invest, or build with top-notch service, I am just a quick text away! Cheers to a wonderful holiday season and a prosperous New Year!

Warmest wishes,
[Your Name]
[Your Brokerage]

Handling Objections

The scripts below are ways you can respond to common objections that clients have. You can copy & paste these into an email or text, or practice saying something similar in person or over the phone.

Objection #1 (Buyer): "I'm Just Browsing"

Hey there! That's totally fine—browsing is actually a great way to get a feel for what's out there. You get to see what styles resonate with you, which neighborhoods vibe with your lifestyle, and what home features you're absolutely in love with—or the ones you could do without.

When you're ready to roll & find a house, I've got the professional experience and the lowdown on everything you need to know. Plus, if you stumble upon something that catches your eye, I can provide you with all the details that aren't listed online—the pros, the cons, and the little secrets that only a seasoned agent would know.

Feel free to reach out if you want to discuss potential next steps or if you have any questions about the properties you come across. Happy house hunting!

Objection #2 (Buyer): "I'm going to buy a home without an agent"

Totally get where you're coming from! The idea of tackling the home-buying process on your own is super appealing to a lot of people. You're thinking you'll save on commission and maybe even get a better deal.

But, buying a house is a huge financial decision. It's not just about finding a place and making an offer. There's negotiating, understanding the market, dealing with paperwork, and navigating the closing process, which a lot of people find really overwhelming.

I'm here to help you snag the best deal, avoid regrets, and make sure you're not leaving anything on the table. Plus, I've got access to listings that might not even hit the big websites, giving you a leg up on the competition.

And you may already know this but...the seller typically covers the commission, so all the expertise, advice, and support I provide? It doesn't actually cost you anything extra to have me on your team helping you buy a home!

I'm all for independence and saving where you can, but I also believe in making sure you're protected and informed every step of the way. If you want to chat more about it, I'm here when you're ready!

Take care and whatever you decide, I wish you a smooth home-buying journey! [Your Name]

Objection #3 (Buyer): "How's the market?"

That's the million-dollar question, right?

If you're looking to buy, interest rates and home prices are the big-ticket items we're watching. Right now, [insert current market trends, e.g., "we're seeing a bit of a cooldown from those crazy bidding wars last year," or "it's still pretty competitive, but homes aren't flying off the market in just a day anymore"].

[X market feature] is good news for you!

If you're on the fence about when to jump in, let's chat about what you're looking for and why. There will never be a 100% perfect opportunity to buy. What's more important is finding the right fit for you and your budget!

I'd love to send you over some ideas and houses, what do you think?

Objection #4 (Buyer): "We should have offered more" [losing out on a deal]

I totally get where you're coming from. Missing out on a place you've set your heart on is really frustrating. But let's keep a couple of things in perspective.

First, it's super important not to get caught up in the heat of a bidding war where you end up stretching way past what's comfortable for your budget. It's not just about winning the bid; it's about making sure you don't win a victory now but have regrets later.

Second, the right place at the wrong price is still the wrong place. Our goal is to find you a home that feels like a win financially and emotionally. I've got my ear to the ground for new listings and I'm here to help you analyze the comps and market conditions so that next time, we can go in with a solid offer that's competitive but still keeps your financial health front and center.

So, let's take this as a learning experience, recalibrate, and keep moving forward. We'll find a place where the numbers make as much sense as the floor plan.

Here for you every step of the way!

Objection #5 (Seller): "I'm not in a hurry to sell/move"

I totally get where you're coming from. It's great that you're not feeling pressured to rush this process. Now is an amazing time to sell, however, because of X, Y,

Z. What would be the perfect, dream scenario that could make you change your mind?

There might be a scenario that you can make happen for your clients, so I always ask them! But, if the client isn't ready to move for personal reasons, you don't want to be pushy or aggressive. If the client truly isn't ready to move, I say:

When you're ready to make a move, I'm here! We'll hit the ground running when you decide it's the right moment to proceed. Feel free to reach out when you're ready to chat more about this. I'm here to work with your schedule and make sure this experience is as smooth and stress-free as possible for you.

Objection #6 (Seller): "Zillow says my house is worth X"

It's super common to check out those estimates of Zillow & other websites – they're quick, they're easy, and they're right there at your fingertips. But here's the inside scoop: those numbers can be like taking a wild shot in the dark sometimes.

They're not usually spot-on and in fact, Zillow has even been sued for these numbers being inaccurate.

What I do is a deep dive into the nitty-gritty details in the MLS. I look at the latest home sales, I do a comparative market analysis, and I factor in the one-of-a-kind features of your home. This way, we can come up with a price that's more than just a guesstimate – it's tailored to what buyers are actually willing to pay for a house like yours.

How about we sit down, grab a coffee, and talk numbers? We'll go over what makes your home the gem that it is and land on a price that'll get buyers hyped and get you the deal you deserve.

Find these scripts helpful? I would love to hear about it! Or maybe you have questions?

Send me a DM or tag me on Instagram @brookeecoughlin or on TikTok @brooke-coughlinrealtor

You can also join my real estate agent community at **sheclosesdeals.com/community**

Cheering you on! Let's rise together!
XO
Brooke

Made in United States
North Haven, CT
28 February 2025

66337182R00074